✳ **The Technology of Consciousness**

family history

✳ How to change your religious reality

✳ **Tracking Your Own Spiritual Repertoire**

✳ Gods and Galactics

THE POTENTIAL

✳ Cosmic beings as gods

✳ **Who is God?**

✳ **Churches Today**

✳ A new sense of the Divine Source

✳ Preaching and prayers

✳ Rituals, ceremonies, baptisms, paraphernalia

✳ **God and the Book**

✳ How writing pretends truth

✳ How religious dogma and rules mold us

✳ New commandments

TODAY

✳ **Molding the Masses**

✳ **Women and The Divine**

✳ How religious concepts structure reality

✳ Dissolving god gender

✳ **God and Sexuality**

✳ **Religious Concepts**

✳ New sexual understanding

For Melinda
May your own
evolution
be filled with
laughter & grace.
You are a
gift to us all

Great love,

Chris

The
EVOLUTION
of GOD

The
EVOLUTION
of GOD

CHRIS GRISCOM

LI
PRESS

Santa Fe, New Mexico

LIGHT INSTITUTE PRESS
40 Calle Nizhoni
Galisteo, New Mexico 87540

BOOK DESIGN AND LAYOUT BY JANICE ST. MARIE

First Edition 2008

Library of Congress Control Number: 2007933548

ISBN: 978-0-9772249-1-3

PRINTED IN THE UNITED STATES OF AMERICA

The Evolution of God is dedicated to
my Higher Self who has woven the tapestry of my life
in such a way that I could only ask these questions,
and listen to the answers so brilliantly whispered
into my reality through many Soul friends
who have taught me to see "truth" as experience.
I know deeply in my being
that beyond life and death is the embrace
of the Divine Source—ever evolving.

CONTENTS

PART 3

THE POTENTIAL

The
EVOLUTION
of GOD

TO THE READER

Beloveds,

You are about to embark upon a journey of the Soul. It is a journey without end or even direction. It is more like dropping a rock into a pond and becoming the ripples traveling outward. I hope that these ripples will awaken in you a new kind of freedom to explore the reaches of your consciousness.

It is about God. It is about who we really are. It is about the questions we never ask and the ones that we are afraid to ask.

I am compelled to write this book because there is a powerful knowing inside of me that tells me it is time to speak of these deeply intrinsic energies within all humankind that must be brought forth and cleared so that we can evolve onto a new octave of life.

We are growing by catapultic leaps in every facet of our consciousness. Our bodies are changing to allow more light. Our mental faculties have exploded onto a multidimensional screen of nanoseconds and invisible realities. We have no trouble using a computer that processes almost instantly any command into a coalesced increment of cognizance. We dare dream of traveling beyond our planet, of miracles and magic—but we don't dare touch our god. We don't dare imagine The Divine actually within us—or beyond our own small world of human form.

We are terrified of our powers to heal or manifest. We think of human potential as something relevant to only a special group of unique beings, but the worst is that we cannot seem to allow ourselves to connect directly with our own Divine Source.

Up until now on our planet we have experienced change as a threatening, dangerous and destablizing energy that we resist within our families, our churches and our countries. However, change is what allows us to test the river of life, and find out what benefits the whole and what does not.

Yes, we are in an eternal pulse of evolution—the evolution of our species, our consciousness and our Soul. It is time to sort through all of our belief systems and find the pearls of wisdom, the keys to joyous, ecstatic and free expression of our divinity. We cannot continue with our limited concepts of God. We cannot breed hatred and fear and war in the name of God. We must activate the intelligence of our hearts and—evolve God. This is not a sacrilege; it is our human right—and our responsibility.

Our Divine Source brought us into our bodies. It existed within us long before sacred books were written to guide us, long before we could even conjure the format or dogma of religious discipline. Now, we are called upon to release the old interpretations of what is spiritual and to breathe our first breaths as Divine beings evolved enough to experience the God Source in every moment of our lives.

This book is not a discourse on religion or God. It is a descriptive synopsis on how we have related to our Source and molded God into a being that we ourselves created through our interpretations of subjective experience. It is exactly that subjectivity that would lead to profound truths if we could embrace it as a part of our purpose. We have all had spiritual experiences, but we have judged them inconsequential or wrong. What if we allowed ourselves to experience God in new ways—without fear or censorship?

Let us shed the skin of a snake that no longer fits us!

I speak these words to you, not because I want to blame or disavow or dishonor religion—but because I know that new energies are moving inside of us all and need to be given voice. Herein is my voice. I invite your voice to join mine, and through bravery and Divine inspiration we can partici-pate in*********

"The Evolution of God."

With great respect and love,

CHRIS GRISCOM

EVOLUTION:
THE SPIRAL OF PERFECTION

When I speak of "evolution" in this book, I am not referring to the contentious discussion of whether humans simply evolved as a natural phenomenon, or whether God created humans distinctly as separate from other animals, or even whether our genesis is about intelligent design. They each have something to offer us, but holding them in polarity to each other is too constrictive to advance a holographic perspective of our place in the universe. Let us explore evolution in a more descriptive way.

Evolution is the result of the law of karma—action and reaction, cause and effect. It means that there is a natural motion that permeates all octaves of the universe, which takes in experience and applies it to function and consciousness, thereby altering it. We say that something is evolving if it changes form or adapts or does something that brings newness into its multidimensional world. Each pulse, or wave, or generation carries with it the potential of a shift that alters the original blueprint—with each motion, a change occurs.

The motion of life penetrates a holographic field of energy, absorbing all its facets until it swings out to the periphery and spins itself up into a spiral—the spiral of evolution. It is a virtual digestion and integration of raw material from which something new emerges.

Evolution is not a linear thing, just as time does not actually travel on a continuum, but rather arcs itself so that the energies of what we call the past, swell into the future, which is pressed up against by the present, spilling its contents that have been crystallized from the past. All potential ripples out from the genesis of Source, squeezes itself into matter and then drains back again into the infinite cycle of reconfiguration and renewal.

If we hold the meaning of the word evolution to its developmental purpose of evolving into ever higher and more perfect states, then it becomes a tool of grace in our lives—a spiral of perfection. What an adventure to evolve on all levels of our being. How would we like to evolve our bodies, our consciousness, our relationships, our societies, our planet?

Nothing stays the same—even though we wish vehemently for it to do so—not because of incessant time, but because of endless cosmic creation. All that we know or have ever known as truth or even life, is the result of the Divine creative force that will eternally alter the realities of form and formless alike. Our lives do not remain the same, nor our world, and certainly not our god.

Yet, we resist any inkling of change when it comes to God, as if even a new Divine thought or expression might cast us into a timeless hell of punishment and shame. We dare not conceive of changing something we consider omnipotent, and certainly no religious institution would support such transgression. If the universe is ever changing, why do we think the Divine Source does not also evolve? Is it because our fear of change is so profound that we cling to that one constant in our lives?

Do we really believe that we will be safe if God stays the same for us? If so, our future is doomed and we will surely slip into oblivion—not because God has called an end of time, but because we will have fallen into a perpetually narrowing abyss of blindness. We have been so shielded from the Divine creative force that we cannot imagine a god that moves with us in our own evolutionary orbit. The truth of creation is that it continues onward; even words on a page will change their meaning as they are read and re-read. This is the mystery of consciousness wherein holographic experience synergistically designs truth.

In effect, we have left God back in a time capsule. We have not explored the infinite possibilities of knowing God because of our limited repertoire of consciousness. Our relationship to the god of our cultural inheritance is shrouded by a passionate fanaticism of misplaced loyalty, a contract of everlasting sameness.

There is a stultifying bondage in this unchanging perspective that foreshadows any religious alteration or advancement in us. How did these contracts of fictitious loyalty come into being? —Through the hand of man.

I profoundly appreciate the predicament of religious dogma. To alter the interpretations of the infallible ones, to reinterpret the prophets, would be unthinkable in terms of religious constancy and doctrine. However, to persist in the illusion of an unchanging god is to place a wedge between the mind and the heart of modern believers. Too much has been said about God's mandates in all religions, and not enough has been taught about how to bring our relationship with The Divine into one of grace and joy. The possibility of new perspectives has always met with the threat of exile. The tragedy here is that we have always believed it would be true.

There is the underlying fear and guilt that if we were to change our religious perceptions, we would somehow be committing treachery against our god and our future inclusion in heaven. The power of heaven and hell in our lives is almost immeasurable. It is the ultimate curse of damnation—"Go to Hell!" It is "the fate worse than death" that has been instilled in every child of almost all religions, from the first moments of their cognizant imagery. Hell looms large on our avoidance scale and we would not risk its eternity of dismal repetition for the sake of an uncertain new interpretation of religious truths. Although, I think that we must!

Changing God is an inconceivable idea for most people. We feel the same way about our own relationships. We would rather stay within the status quo than face any change that might put our safe habits and patterns at risk. The power of conformity and religious institutionalization is gigantic! We actually do not realize that we have the power to reinvent ourselves or anybody else. The world is full of relationships merely existing on automatic pilot. Each partner waits for the other to do something that will bring life into routine. It seems unimaginable to contemplate the possibility that we could change God, even though that relationship has never, as yet, approached its full potential. It can not, until we free it from the constrictive prison of the human mind.

Though we travel the world and witness many different forms of spiritual expression, if we consider changing our religion, or even in some areas, our church, we may be forced through grueling hoops of familial and social disapproval that threaten us with subtle ostracism. The strength of our religious convictions is anchored into the places we worship and the people who go there with us. Familiarity, packed with all the sensations of sight, sound and smell that impregnate memory, tethers us to a stylized God. Even the great masses of people who no longer espouse to believe in religion, find themselves in a kind of suspended animation when they come into contact with the religious paraphernalia of their past. As we evolve God, the structures, icons, and all other symbolic representations will have to be changed. Imagine Christian churches without crosses!

It is not enough to stagnate in the past because history claims its limited version of truth, or our preachers and parents say we must. We have new faculties of mind and spirit. We can now reexamine our spiritual history and see clearly the influences of collective consciousness that have shaped our religious worlds.

Elements of fear and hatred have been bred into that history because of the darkness of mind possessed by our primordial ancestors. They saw only the black and white of reality—life and death. They painted karmic action and reaction in the extremes of heaven and hell. They did not fully comprehend the hologram of unending universes through which the past and future converge; and life, death and rebirth pursue each other in concentric ripples of evolutionary expansion.

Religious evolution merged out of the loosely woven fabric of tribal life that became cultural societies and kingdoms wrapping themselves around the communal expression, worship, and ultimately, the far-reaching politics—of God.

We can see the laws of karma at work when we view the action and reaction sequences of spiritual endeavors as they evolved into religions with specific formulas, rituals and dogmas that described their belief systems. The rigid backbone of religious belief supplied the pretext for the wars that victimized one group, who in turn became the victimizers. Territories were conquered and then overthrown as allies expediently altered their loyalties—back and forth into the present.

Even the concept of karma needs an evolutionary adjustment in terms of today. In Eastern vernacular, karma has always represented a more negative and fatalistic perspective through which we are punished for our misdeeds in other lifetimes. If we fall off the edge of goodness, we will pay through the laws of karma—now or later. This perspective is only a surface view of the law of karma, which refers to all energies—both thought and deed, positive and negative. Karma can be a wonderful magnetic convergence of miraculous events through the lineage of good deeds. "Like attracts like" is one way to describe it, or "you reap what you sow" is another expression that finds its place in many religious teachings. The latter expression is usually spoken in the context of punishment for doing wrong, rather than its powerful inspiration that all good action returns to you "tenfold."

Our forefathers could perceive the force of ancestry dictating their lives in terms of the limits of choice and possibility, but they could not fathom how the experiences and thoughtforms of their relatives intrinsically shaped their destiny. They did not know that experience has life; that it becomes an unspoken blueprint passed on from one to another through the psychogenetics of blood, culture and spirit. This is something still on the horizon of our consciousness; a seed I am compelled to plant in hopes of contributing to a catapultic leap in human potential.

Spiritual DNA is an illusive bundle of innuendos hovering over the more palpable physical and emotional DNA. Together, they are interwoven into a cohesive whole that whispers back and forth across the veil of the unmanifest and completes the composition of who we are. As we will see later, our spiritual DNA is not locked into the matrix of one body, one lifetime, or even our human form. From our family constellation we have inherited an almost infinite palate of color and texture that paints our religious world. We have also inherited levels of spiritual wisdom and grace that seem to be still latent, and yet are beginning to awaken universally, in all humans.

Though the spiritual and religious experiences of our fore-fathers are indelibly imprinted within the psychogenetic confines of our DNA, we can become aware of those deep historic grooves to perceive how we ourselves have repeated them! This is not an uplifting thought, but if we are brave enough to peer into the black hole of the past, we will be spared any temptation to descend into its darkness or go there again. When we reopen the past sleeves of historical religion, we can see the trickery—and know that we are beyond it now. Through the power of enlightened consciousness, we can virtually mend and replace the weakest strands of our spiritual templates. Evolution will carry us onward to a more gentle and loving embrace of The Divine.

As we follow this circuitous path of the God Force in our history, we can see that its religious tentacles did, indeed, wind around and through all aspects of our lives. These tentacles were laden with the sticky pretext of what God wanted—then, even as now. God was the excuse for war, thievery, torture, and the thirst for power. It was the untouchable voices of religious leaders who called for those wars, who played with lives and kingdoms like a game of chess. All too much residue of intrigue and treachery is still with us. It is time to untether God from all our excuses.

Despite the claims ferociously shouted from pulpits around the world, God "wants" nothing, "needs" nothing from humans. To preach to the contrary is a fallacy of manipulation. We are here on this earth to evolve spiritually. That is our mandate—to become conscious, enlightened beings. It is the gift we give back to our creator, the only one of any significance. It is not that some personal god force demands it from us, it is that the natural force of evolution brings it to us—even when we do not consciously seek it.

Our spiritual evolution must not be restricted to a historical lineage alone. We have recorded it in terms of time and the events that make it real to us, but this is not the whole story. We are not the victims of our religious history, we are the survivors who must now clear the debris and begin again. We were given the gift of "free will" that bestows upon us the power to choose for ourselves; this spiritual freedom is intrinsic to the evolution of consciousness. The higher our consciousness, the more the energetic arch that returns to the Divine Source affects its own evolution. Negative consciousness of fear and destruction would not meet the frequency of the God Source, it would only reverberate within lower octaves.

As strange as it may seem, when new realities begin to dawn there is an arousal of all the negative and past energies that must be cleared to make room for the new. It is a duel to the death between that which was and that which will be. This is exactly why we look out on the world today and see such violence and strife. Our earth is like a sponge that has absorbed all of human history that has been played out upon it. The tribe against tribe, the battlefields, the hatred and the fear are all oozing up to be released.

These eruptions do not signify the end of the world as the fear mongers would have us believe; they are the mechanisms of release that precede all new cycles. In fact, we cannot reach a new cycle without them because they are the blockages that sabotage our will to evolve. Look at the places that are most entrenched in this upheaval—Africa and the Middle East. They are the focal points for these clearings because of the permeation of human experience that have passed through them. Their land and their people are laden with the lives and experiences of thousands of years. We cannot go that way again, and yet we cannot go on until those energies have been transmuted. Every one of us holds crystallizations of these places and energies—either through blood, psychogenetic imprinting or incarnations of the Soul.

We must release all the places on this earth that hold these residues so that they are not repeated. Otherwise, it is like the tiger chasing its tail—around and around in the exhausting circle of repetition. We can do this—we have the technology of consciousness to advance, and we can do it together. It is exactly what I am sharing with you in this book. Because of it, a new cycle will begin—and it begins with us. (Please see Chapter 11, *Tracking Your Own Spiritual Repertoire* and Chapter 12, *Technology of Consciousness*.)

Let's peruse your religious façade for a moment so that you can begin this process of conscious awareness. Perhaps you innately and secretly dislike people from another religion without really knowing why. Probably, you hide your feelings because it is "unenlightened" to admit to such a prejudice, but it nevertheless lurks about, under the surface. If so, you can be sure that you are carrying a seed of hatred bred by your blood relatives through their experiences, which has passed into you—even if it all occurred hundreds or thousands of years ago. This is an amazing illumination.

We are born with the predilections of our forefathers!

You may have inherited a certain character predilection from one of your distant relatives who held very rigid beliefs about God. Not only might you tend to manifest those character attributes of rigidity and intolerance, but also you might find yourself looking at others from different religious backgrounds with disdain and judgment—without even being aware that you are doing it. Since we fear God, we fear any other religious adherents that practice their religion differently than we. Deep belief systems are so intrinsic to us that we don't recognize their fallacies. We unconsciously qualify them as absolute truth, and they rarely surface into the questioning mind.

Not all of your spiritual background is negative. You can be sure that somewhere in your family constellation you have relatives who had profound and joyous spiritual experiences. They may have felt the mystery of Divine presence in their life. Imagine the possibilities of piggybacking on those ecstatic foundations to blissful and all-embracing connections of your own! Even if that tale has not been passed down in your family, even if that person never shared what happened with anyone else, you can access it through your psychogenetic encoding. (Please see my book, *Psychogenetics: The Force of Heredity.*)

You may have a strong feeling for a certain religion, its cornucopia of images, smells and sounds that intrigue you or open you up to some profound place of recognition. They may all be encapsulations of experiences that have been passed into you through genetic pathways. Your sense acuity connects you to memories and emotions that heighten your energetic antennae.

Allow yourself to expand into the realms of reincarnation. Your infinite repertoire of bodies, cultures, and spiritual experiences are still feeding the essence of your being. Memories imprint themselves very deeply in the mind of the cell and are carried indefinitely within us, creating points of association and reference that trigger flashes of inexplicable emotion. In short, you may have inherited from yourself, a powerful predilection of religious sensibilities that are still moving in your cells at this very moment!

Time has absolutely no power over the astral residues imprinted psychogenetically within us. So often, we really do not understand our loathing and hatred of others who practice different forms of worship than ourselves. We are rarely told the stories of our family constellation who went before us in different times and places that would illuminate their religious experiences—yet those very experiences may be shaping our lives! Were they perpetrators of harm onto those of other religions? Did they silently and fearfully suffer discrimination by people who saw them only through their religious affiliation? The answers to these queries are buried with our forefathers and our own spiritual DNA. We can find them through conscious exploration into the illusive templates of spiritual inheritance.

Blend all of this into the multitude of opinions you have about the world and you will begin to see that some of your thoughtforms aren't really yours, and have not come from your own experiences. It does not mean that your ancestors are to blame for your distrust or prejudice towards others, it simply means that you are carrying psychogenetic imprints that influence your subjective conclusions about the world around you. Ultimately, you cannot embrace your own truth until you sort out what is yours and what is not.

Without the microscope of spiritual introspection we cannot discover our own part in these outer realities. When we have delineated our spiritual inheritance, we will have more tools to help us divest ourselves of the religious burdens our forefathers laid upon us—paving the way for a new spiritual foundation that we can joyously pass on to the future.

EVOLUTION

1. That which would create the karmic balancing of our spiritual repertoire would be for all religions to embrace each other so that the past misdeeds perpetrated one upon another would be dissolved from the spiritual DNA of the entire human race.

PART ONE

Primordial Awareness

Forces of Nature
Become the
Embodiment of God

ONE

CREATING GOD:
FEAR, TO SACRIFICE,
TO BLAME, TO GUILT

WE NEED TO TALK ABOUT GOD! We need to sift through eons of imprints that imprison us within the confines of thoughtforms that do not hold true in our present arena of existence. This conversation about God needs to be a new kind of conversation, not the inane rambling about whose side "he" is on, how he will punish us or the way we must live or worship, but something much more profound—how God evolves and what it could mean to us to view our Divine Source from the perspective of its own evolution. Again, I am not talking about the kind of evolution that occurs in nature as opposed to the concept of Divine intention—I am talking about the fact that the entirety of unimaginable universes streams on throughout the galaxies in infinite variation and combination to render time helpless to compete with its ebb and flow of creation. As this is so, it must follow that the Divine Source also evolves and transforms to allow the chorus of infinity to sing new worlds—and new life.

The laws of energy do not describe a force that travels on in isolation without interplay to other energies. Einstein taught us the laws of relativity through which we can realize that all matter and non-matter are connected. Imagine the probability that the creator is itself touched by its creation as the energy streams out and returns impregnated by expression and experience through the fabric of interconnectedness, which then alters the potential of them both. Our relationship with God is not one directional, it is the dance of life.

First we saw God as a force of nature, then a complexity with many faces, and then we saw God as a creator represented and expressed through the male, human form. Now it is time to exponentially revise God into a consciousness that can help us to touch it even within the formless; to know that it is we, ourselves, who sculpt the form and voice of God in accordance with what we can perceive. God itself does not mind the form we choose, but inhabits all matter and non-matter alike. As does the rain love to rain, the wind to blow, God is God within all energetic and material realms.

Our perception is exploding onto a horizon of brilliant palette and craves a new view of God—one without the smallness of human manipulation and projection—one which has integrated the magnificent teachings brought to humanity through all the prophets, seers and saints who have experienced or have been bestowed illumination through Divine focus.

We have come into a world of constant and driving change. The era of information opens us up to new dilemmas about who we are and what we should think and feel about our world. Many of our old beliefs simply do not stand up to scientific scrutiny or logical reality. On the one hand, science itself is embarrassed by its own fluctuation of yesterday's "proven" theories and today's revised truths, while on the other hand, our most solemn religions demand we pretend the messages given in the old worlds must be as true for us today as they were thousands of years ago. This stagnation has become lethal to our willingness to invite religions into our daily reality. Rather, there is a deadly separation between our relationship to God and what we do and feel in our lives.

Every new era must devise new forms of communion with the Divine Source so that the illumination furthers the advancement of our species. At some point in our own evolution as humans, our relationship to the Divine Source needs to go beyond commandments about what not to do in our lives, but how to quicken our frequencies so we can put in action the powers that transcend the density of our villainous history. We are in that process at this very moment, and we are finding it very difficult to let go without experiencing a sense of betrayal.

Caught in residues of old belief systems and culture patternings, we feel guilty because we espouse to be true to our religions, and yet we live in a different kind of reality that is often in direct opposition to the teachings we were born into through our families and cultures. Perhaps today we more have faith in our religions than believe in them. Faith allows us to feel something when we enter a church or celebrate a holiday, and to embrace those feelings with awe and mystery without question. Belief asks us to bend intellect to pretend something is true when we may clearly see that it could not literally be so.

"Do you believe in God?" they say—
"Yes," you mutter—"Of course!"
We know God exists, but that belief comes from our undiscerning faith.

In effect, we compartmentalize God into the unseen areas of our lives, since in most situations it is not socially permissible to mention God or religion in any public way. Privately, we are confused and uncomfortable except in the institutionalized patterns in which we participate by performing sanctioned motions of reverence—on automatic pilot. There are few enraptured audiences in church these days. Look around and you will detect the strain of patience during sermons, the flinch of guilt and head bowed in religious shame, but not the passion of joy to be focused on the Divine Source.

We have gone to extreme lengths to deny our connection to The Divine itself. We often use the name of God as an expression of frustration and to wield the power of damning— "God damn you!" In moments of helplessness and anger, we use the word God as a swear word. "God, I hate that," or "Jesus Christ!" How is it that God became the verbal attachment to all that is out of sync in our lives?

We have been taught by our religions that the worst sin is to think ourselves holy or touched by God. Why? The psychogenetic residue of Christian Crusades, witch-hunts, Muslim holy wars and ethnic cleansings has scarred our spiritual template. It would seem more natural to acknowledge that everyone could have spontaneous spiritual experiences that allow us our sense of worthiness to relate to God. Instead, we set difficult initiations of will, corporal punishment or denial, and interminable rituals of recitation to convince ourselves, and each other, that we are worthy of a Divine relationship—one that is already inextricable between ourselves and our creator—whether we are criminal or saint.

We mostly keep the experience of God at a safe distance so we don't have to confront our sense of guilt that we are not who we say we are. Where did this guilt come from? Why is it so deeply engrained in our lives and cultures? Certainly our religions are permeated with the stench of guilt. All religious authorities perpetrate guilt because it is so very effective for controlling the masses. It is time to strip this negativity from our spiritual and carnal realities, as well as from the preachers who wield it as a weapon over us.

In truth, God began as a concept of fierce power that struck us down when we displeased it. Those early imprints are still within us, locked away in the psychogenetic encoding of our unconscious selves. The fear of God weighs so heavily upon us that we have not yet dared to truly explore the deepest truth—that we are each and all a part of the Divine spark. Just as our children carry our attributes, so do we carry those of God. We have not fully understood the qualities of love and compassion that we can experience through the Divine template, and thus our world seems devoid of the goodness that was bestowed upon us through our spiritual DNA.

In the arena of fast technology we can clone and grow life, but we cannot initiate life. There is something all-encompassing and infinite that lends life to us. We cannot create that spark ourselves, but we can use it. We have arrived at a pivotal moment in which we can use life in an entirely new way. This is exactly why we exist. In fact, we must become the powerful and loving beings of our Divine human template, or we will destroy ourselves.

What does it mean to be created by the Divine spark? It means that we are here, in body, to be the vehicle of expression of a universal Soul. It means that we are perfect and imbued with all the beauty, power and Divine energies that are the essence of what we call God. What would it look like to live in such a way that our thoughts and actions were permeated with a sense of Divine purpose? It would be easy to love, to be compassionate, to discover the power of free will, and above all, to experience the bliss of belonging. It is this hunger to belong that binds us so tenaciously to our cultural religious expressions that seem to have so little meaning for many people outside of the link to a place in us that holds the comfort of belonging.

Beyond this mundane connection, we **do** belong to a universal energy that permeates universes beyond universes. In our lifetime, we will witness that opening into a cosmic arena, which will alter our concept of God and teach us new truths about life—we are not alone in the infinite sea of cosmic currents. Humans are group animals. We are taught and seek our place within our communal world. Our myopic view of God causes us to insist that God look and act like us. How incredibly illusionary and destructive is this view of the infinite Divine Source.

In our desperation to belong, we have created a force of belonging shoved up against the frightening wall of not belonging. Thus, we leer at those who do not belong to "our" god/religion. We call them names and battle them, not so much because of *themselves*, but because they threaten our sense of place. Who belongs? Does God have a place for others? Would the creator of all humans really choose one group over another? Each group, religion, or culture clutches desperately to the illusion that no other groups have God's favor, that all others have displeased God and so deserve to be driven out.

The fear and hatred that has been engendered between our religions and our gods comes from our profound confusion as to who we are. It is our historical habit to wield God as a weapon in our battle with others as if our relationship to God would be threatened by the possibility that God would love them too. If we want to feel loved by God all we have to do is give love to our Divine Source by seeing and experiencing it in everything and everybody in our third dimensional world. This is not as difficult as it appears, and the practice of love is the fastest way to free us from our relationship addictions of jealousy and ownership that we so deftly transfer from God to each other.

Perhaps this statute of envy is the source of all the sibling rivalry we experience today. God has been painted as the disapproving parent whose favor we must attain—no matter what. In the same way that we identify ourselves through our parents, we identify through our relationship to our god that is ingrained in us by our religious upbringing—even when we espouse to have none. The outcome of this psychogenetic pattern is rebellion—which is exactly the state of things in today's world of religion.

We don't want an angry god/parent anymore. In actuality, we have outgrown this stultifying totem pole form of relating. We don't want to jump through the hoops of fire in order to be worthy of heaven. We don't want to be unworthy—period!

The best way to do this is to sift through and discard the negative concepts we hold about ourselves, and our god. As the albatross is lifted there will be a natural evolution of consciousness through which we can perceive the Divine Source in the light of expanded truth. Perhaps if we return to our initial awareness of God consciousness, we can more clearly see how those early perceptions have set us up for the irrational and destructive way our negative religious concepts have forged us into the fearful, guilty, shameful and un-illuminated cast of characters we seem to be today.

Nature gave no favors to primordial humans. Volcanoes spewed lava and rock onto a virgin world and imprinted on early humans their inconsequential smallness. Caught in that landscape of constant danger, survival necessitated a vigilant tuning of the instinctual faculties to the sounds and movements in the periphery that might bring death at any moment.

Nature herself was full of intense and frightening energies that engendered awe and fear. From the sky descended showers of rain, snow, wind, and cycles of heat and cold that etched the landscape into a myriad of challenges for the early humans. As our ancestors interacted with their world, they began to recognize a force of creation that seemed to hurl its power directly at them. When there was a storm or eruption, a trembling, or a great wind, they interpreted it as a personal act focused on them.

Hold in your mind a moment the devastating images of the recent tsunamis, the hurricane, Katrina, the sight of whole villages crumbling to the ground, and you can enter into their world of abject horror. Imagine this force of nature rushing at you. There is nothing impersonal or accidental about it! There is just you and this raging power locked in the embrace of death, and instinctually you cry out for mercy.

All the fear and confusion our forefathers experienced at the mercy of nature is stored within our own cellular memory. Through the pathways of psychogenetic imprinting, their realities live on in us encoded into our physical, emotional and spiritual DNA. Perhaps that is why we so fear the dark, the fires, the waters of our world and why we are caught spellbound by them; and at the same time, wish so vehemently to override those forces of nature.

The instant our ancestors pleaded for their lives, they embarked upon an evolutionary leap of consciousness. It was a new awareness of the self and the other, and it brought with it the possibilities of relationship that are innate to our human species today. Suddenly, there were all the questions and perceptions about other beings that advanced their collective reality. Like their own explosions of fear and anger, they projected those energies of nature onto this colossal power that held their existence in its grip, and they gave it the name—GOD.

Once they had named this force, everything looked and felt different to them. In a flash of comprehension they saw that they could participate, or at least influence, the kind of energy God was extending. Emboldened by this possibility, they set about negotiating their survival and devising ways to please the omnipotence that surrounded them. The extent of their capacities to relate to each other, and subsequently to their God, was very rudimentary and crude.

Enthralled with this new relationship adventure, they began to interpret the gamut of nature's attributes as separate entities. They embraced a god of rain, a god of hunting, a god of fertility. Each god had a certain kind of power that had to be reckoned with. The reckoning took the form of trying to ascertain what the gods wanted in return for the rain or food or protection that they implored them to give. Our forefathers surmised that the gods needed to be placated so that they would not turn their forces against them or destroy them, but would help them to survive. They feared the gods—whose anger became the cause of all danger.

Initially, the ancients did not recognize these gods as their Source or creators. They did not feel related to them, nor could they dream that they were created by them, but rather experienced them as forces outside themselves. Since our ancestors had no awareness of biological functions, they did not know where life came from. They thought the gods bestowed and controlled life, but they did not think themselves "sons of God." They might have imagined God as a bolt of lightning, a volcano or even a dragon, but not a god in human form; that projection came much later when we began to attempt to override nature.

It is interesting to note that in most creation myths we assigned to the gods very human emotional characteristics such as anger, jealousy, egotism, vengeance, judgment, and desire. Throughout the human epics on this planet, we have personalized the world around us in such a way that everything seems to be about us, and we project our own realities onto that world. Since truth is seen only from our eyes, it appears one directional. Whatever we are, is also our view of all else. This has left us with a relationship to our God Force that is not whole, not peaceful—but wrought with expectations and disappointment.

From the very beginning, the supplication and placation of the gods became a crucial part of life, and at some point in this process, one of the group began to take on the role of intermediary to the gods. Perhaps that man may have felt God spoke to him. He could have guessed correctly at a future event, or in the midst of some natural upheaval had a vision that cast him into a position of leadership. Since nothing was more crucial than harmony with the gods, he became the most important person in the tribe. He himself was given a title that described his special status in the tribe. He might have been called the mogul, the shaman, the priest—whatever it was, he took the power of choosing for the tribe, and was therefore given many powers of privilege.

In his all-encompassing role of God pleaser, he had to find ways to make the gods happy with him. He learned to not only give offerings to the gods, but in an attempt to ensure that the offerings were acceptable, he began to sacrifice life to them, as well. Animals, and ultimately humans, became the victims of sacrifice. He did not see that he was killing God's own creation.

This is a hugely important point! Our ancestors concluded God wanted and demanded repayment for life—that God ensnared the priest in an unending cycle of sacrificial demonstrations of fidelity and submission. What are the psychogenetic conclusions of this act reverberating in us now?

- That we must bargain for our lives
- That sacrifice will save us
- That God must be placated
- That we are unworthy
- That sacrifice is the way to God

The ramifications of this relationship through sacrifice are still rippling out around the world today—the suicide bombers, the penitents, the sheep of Ramadan, the dark rites of cults, the bloody alters...

All the while, if we could look back and see that it started in the mind of MAN—not God—we would be able to use our higher consciousness to change something that is not true.

God never asked for sacrifice!!!!!

Only the machinations of primordial man could see this sacrificial mandate as true. Many early religions upheld the existence of a god of destruction. That concept arose from the mentality of a barely conscious group of humans at the dawn of time. That era of human existence was filled with the darkness of survival and the dangers of primitive perception.

The Old Testament tells the story of Abraham in which God asks him to destroy his son as a test of his loyalty and obedience to him. An all-powerful god would not need to test Abraham. This is a story of a lesser, more insecure being. As the true creator, all the intricacies of the human template would be known. The scenario calling for a personification of an ungodly personality, demanding violence and death in the name of God could only come from the mind of man. Why would God ask for the destruction of its own creation?

No one will ever know how this story of Abraham actually came into being. Was it the imagination of a confused old man, thinking God was talking to him? Even what we know about him is secondhand. His story was certainly one according to his time—not ours.

Some renditions of this story say that God wanted Abraham to prove his "love" for him. The test was that Abraham must show that he loved God over his son by killing the competing object of Abraham's affection. Whether it was obedience, love, loyalty or something else, it has fed the demon of negativity that continues to stalk us today. Even among ourselves, we use this weapon of "proof" in our relationships. "If you love me, you will…"

Our entire human race is polluted with the psychogenetic poison of quantitative and "comparative" love. No one could ever love two people exactly in the same way, because of the infinite Soul repertoire that shadows our relationships with projections and associations that are unique between any two people.

How many children have suffered under this cruel attempt to extract equal love? We constantly expose them to these concepts from the very beginning by presuming that each additional child will "take away" love from the others. Most children secretly feel less loved by their parents, which they later project onto their spouses and children, and thus perpetuate the comparative love syndrome into the shadowy future.

In each lifetime we love handfuls of people—every one of them in a different way. There are interweaving qualities of love such as parental love, friendship love, sexual love, and sacred love that color and give unique texture to our love relationships. They are each a magical mix of alchemy and cannot be duplicated or shared from one to another.

Many of these biblical stories could be interpreted not as how we should do what was allegedly done thousands of years ago, but as illuminating reference points into the psyche of our human ancestors; and how the laws of behavior and structures of society were formed into cohesive increments of reality through instructional stories passed down verbally and filtered by the degree of limited enlightenment of those who told them. If they had not been laced by the emotional, mental and spiritual shortcomings of their perpetrators, we would not be so burdened with such constrictive and negative choices today. It is left to us to discover that there are other solutions to our dilemmas—other perceptions that offer us clarity and more holographic awareness. Hopefully, we have grown beyond the problem solving capacities of our forefathers.

Mental institutions today are filled with people who insist that God speaks to them. If you thought God were asking you to sacrifice your child as proof of loyalty, I assure you that you would be diagnosed as mentally ill and dangerous. How would we determine the validity of God speaking to someone today? Why do we feel that only in the olden times did God talk to us?

It is as if all authenticity were frozen in a time capsule thousands of years old. Perhaps it is because so little was recorded that each "testament" has been given a vote of truth simply because it eluded the veils of time. My answer to the question of authentication of God's voice would be that if you felt great energies of compassion and oneness during the transmission of the message, heard words of love and inspiration, you might be tapping into the universality of the God Source.

**God never gave a franchise to a selected few.
You have the birthright of direct experience!**

Our perception of our freedom to connect directly with the
God Force has never yet surfaced due to the early usurpation
of that power by the moguls and priests. Imagine the responsibility of protecting the survival of a whole tribe! The shaman
had to find ways to intercede on our behalf; to ask for what
we needed and to bargain with the gods over our place in
the natural scheme of things. If some catastrophe struck, the
tribe might lose faith in his powers and perhaps even punish
or cast him out. No priest could risk that, so he had to invent
possible and terrifying outcomes if his people did not obey
him. Our present day fear of God's wrath was imprinted in
our human psyche from the very darkly shadowed beginning.
Down the eons of time has come the residue of those early
"God brokers" who chose to do it themselves.

How did the shaman/priest get his people to agree to let someone die for God? First, he used the power of fear to prove the
necessity of sacrifice, i.e., God would be angry and direct the
forces of nature against them all. Then he convinced them
that only the best could be sacrificed, only the holy could be
chosen, only the victim could receive special favors—before
and after death. These acts were born of desperate tactics and
under the pretense of the all-powerful spiritual leaders, to
ensure the lives of their tribe and their own.

In this instant of human history the force of **blame** took hold
as an attribute of responsibility, and with it came the avoidance of being faulted. How did the shaman protect himself
from such vulnerability? He created templates of behavior,

rules to be followed that were designed to please the gods. If something went wrong, he could put the blame on his people for not doing exactly what he told them to do, or for being impure or innately unworthy to God. From this moment there came an arbitrary system of judging who was "good" and who was "not good" in the eyes of God and the shaman. Virtually every major religion still uses some part of this blame, to guilt, to unworthy repertoire.

Aren't these the same ploys utilized today to motivate suicide bombers, penitentes, and the righteous lambs of God to engage in inhuman acts before an angry God? These weapons of persuasion are the mandates forged by those early priests who imprinted us with such profound unworthiness that we hardly dare even wonder what it would be like to be the priest ourselves.

The externalization of power has left us with the limp conclusion that we are not strong enough to manage our lives alone and that only something or someone outside us can insure our safety, our survival, and even our choice to use our human abilities. In this decisive moment of our psychogenetic evolution, we created inner and outer worlds. We formed the illusion of separate forces and began to see reality from a vertical perspective, a totem pole of highest to lowest, and based on these placements of value, we inserted ourselves into the structures of power—well beneath those who could whisper to God.

The word "power" evokes fervent emotional reactions in us all. In one moment it could carry the energy of pride. In another moment, it could be vengeance, or control, or fear.

When it comes to God, certainly fear and anger are the two most prevalent associations that freeze our freedom to change and evolve.

Fear is the most powerful tool of conformity—even today. The concept that God must be feared has become a way of speaking about someone as a truly good person. In many churches they say, "He is God-fearing," meaning that he can be trusted and is worthy. Our assumption is that if you fear God, you will not step out of bounds—fearing God pleases God. Unfortunately, without the stretching, the questioning, and the experiencing we may never come to know God in new ways; ways that heal us, teach us and give us the strength to evolve ever closer to godliness ourselves.

I am certain that an "almighty" God would not need reassurance of its power through the fear responses of mere humans. Our perpetual fears of God were spawned in the ponds of primordial manipulation. It was self-serving then, and it is today.

It is not God who needs our compliance and obedience; it is the fabrication of our religions to bind us into a matrix of unified servitude.

To the sword of fear we can add the wound of anger. The church threatens with fear and then drives that sword so deeply into the human psyche that we are almost mortally wounded by the cut of God's anger and wrath. Most religions utilize this weapon of anger to hold their followers in check.

Anger is a yang (external) energetic. It always covers fear, a yin (internal) immobilizing contraction. This means that the louder and angrier the shouts, the more fear crouches beneath them. The god of Abraham and Isaiah has always been portrayed as an angry god. His image emerged from a dark swamp of fear that could not conceive of true peace.

Who told us these stories? —Man. Who instilled the mythology of the angry God? —Man. Our trembling repertoire of God experiences has been about repentance versus resplendent joy—death into hell, rather than Divine life. It is time to awaken from this nightmare and recreate our god—and ourselves.

Now that we know how we came to fear God, we can lay down the burdens of sacrifice, unworthiness, and guilt we carried for so long and purge ourselves of these old perceptions of God, so that we can continue our own evolution into higher octaves of reality.

 "God is love" I was taught. That never included fear or punishment. The fact is that no one really loves the thing they fear. God's love is without blame or conformity. Allow yourself to receive it and the whole human race will spin upward!

EVOLUTION

1. Release your image of God. Let go of the form that you were taught represents God.

2. Imagine a thousand years into the future. What is your first perception of the god form? If it is inspiring, allow yourself to take that image into your body.

3. Contemplate what conclusions you have inherited about pleasing God. Release them. (See Chapter12, *Technology of Consciousness.*)

4. Dissolve your fear of God. (See Chapter12, *Technology of Consciousness.*)

5. Open your consciousness to experience a communion with God.

TWO

EVOLVING INTO RELIGIONS

W E MUST DWELL A BIT MORE on our religious beginnings, because it is vital to comprehend how human suffering and pain became a part of our spiritual and daily reality. Through the lens of the past, we can see how this has been a point of repetition that has followed us into today. "History repeats itself," the historians tell us, and it always will until we become conscious of its presence in our deepest genetic essence.

As the sacrificial pattern took root into the lives of our ancestors, the collective consciousness embraced it as an integral part of existence. Early humans moved to the sacrificial ceremonies of appeasement and supplication to their gods by performing these acts as rituals of prescribed repetition. Those "chosen" to be offered up for sacrifice were not summarily tossed into the volcano or the cenote of water, but were "prepared" to meet the God Force by their priests. There is evidence that in some religious sacrificial rituals, the victims were drugged or numbed; a numbness that resembles our religious thought patterns today. (We do not seek to know God in new ways, instead we go through the motions on automatic pilot.)

We do not seem to question the deepest premise of our religions—that the God Force did, indeed, talk to a handful of men thousands of years ago, and has hardly spoken since. What was told to them was very little about God, but a lot about how to live as humans.

We cannot even surmise what the chosen human sacrificial offerings were told. Did the priests whisper to them that all the others would be safe because of them? Did they think their angry god would be kind to them because they had been sacrificed? Were they instructed that there was an afterlife in some kind of special place? Where they told there would be conscious awareness after leaving their bodies? Perhaps many of our own mythologies about heaven and hell are rooted to these primordial beginnings.

The concept of dying for God would never have been successful without skillful manipulation by the early priests. They had to create some form of enticement or even fear in their chosen offerings to perform the sacrifice. Certainly, for those whose lives were already smothered by poverty and hopelessness, the hook was more palpable.

Not only was sacrifice included in their lives, but later on it came to command some reverence for those who took it upon themselves to enact any such gestures. Self-sacrifice came into being as a part of the early rituals, and continued to find creative expression through self-flagellation and other forms of physical punishment. All these self-tortures were based on varied interpretations of God's approval through pain and suffering. It is unfathomable to me that we are still holding the same conclusions today—that pain and suffering are valid ways to become close to God, who is always watching our individual actions.

Somewhere in the conversation between man and God there came a crossover of identity in which God became the energy and image of a father figure. It was the beginning of personalizing the God Force into a truly direct relationship. It coalesced into a male vibration and we addressed it as "He." The physical strength and dominance of males made it logical to perceive God in the same way. It is much easier to relate to God in an arena we recognize and "God, the Father" helped us to believe that our emissaries could indeed speak to **him**.

When Christianity arrived on the scene, we had a perfect model for self-sacrifice in Jesus. We crystallized our perspective of him as the one who was beaten and who carried the heavy cross that was to become the vehicle of his death. What a frenzy of bodily abuse ensued from the psychogenetic imprint of that cross!

Sacrificial practice has bred several shadowy renditions of its morbid self. Primarily, it gave birth to martyrdom, which still holds us in its treacherous spell today. Because those who suffered death at the hands of their faith did so from such a place of seeming purity and even zeal, we have been inspired by their fates. I wonder what they would have told us about it themselves. Sadly, martyrdom has claimed its place of validity in all the human cultures of the present. It is so insidious that we have woven it into the fabric of emotional subjectivity without even being aware of it.

To be the "martyr" is to be the victim of life, circumstance, or even God. Victimization is a very secure niche in which we can feel safe from the danger of responsibility—it is not our fault, we didn't do it. Coupled with blame and excuse, we can pretend ourselves small and innocent against the onslaught of our world. Because too few of us have been taught about karma (cause and effect), synchronicity, and spiritual laws, we do not see our part in all experience. My Higher Self says that **"the victim and the victimizer are one."** That means there is a spiritual connection between all beings and events. We cannot see this correlation from a mental or emotional point of view. We can only recognize it when we expand our consciousness into more enlightened realms. Why is one a victim and another, not? Is it an accident, a coincidence, a quirk of fate? No. It has meaning. When we learn to seek the purpose, we become free from the victimization and find our infinite strength. At The Light Institute, we say, "What is the Gift?" Search for the teaching in all situations and you will discover your true self.

In exchange for suffering, we are often given an almost universal sympathy that comes with being the victim. We associate sympathy with love and comfort—energies that we desperately long for in our lives. Most all religions teach the virtue of sympathy, whereas in actuality, sympathy is a debilitating offering that holds the victim in a place of helplessness and justification of their impotence—in the face of powers bigger than themselves. Empathy, on the other hand, allows one to understand and care for another, while at the same time being conscious that their misfortune can be overcome. In effect, no one is a "poor thing," but rather a powerful Soul who has the courage to learn a lesson, balance a karma, or pass through an initiation that will free them and others, from a spiritual and energetic blockage. They are the victims only because they are not aware of what is actually happening— and their part in it.

We may not always take martyrdom to the extreme of life or death, but we have learned to finesse the illusion of great sacrifice of ourselves for others. In this way we have the pretexts we need to skirt the shame of not becoming as successful and powerful as we think is expected of us. Almost any role can be played out as one in which we have had to give up what we wanted at great cost—a mother for her child, a man for his family…

Feeling the martyr is actually very satisfying for many people. Why do we set ourselves up to be martyrs? It is a seed intrinsically nurtured by the illusion that suffering makes one holy. Our collective imprints of sin and guilt cause us to feel that we must allow retribution. Martyrdom is a fluke of misinformation about our relationship with ourselves as well as with God. We need not aspire to a life of justification—one in which we punish ourselves through others who cause us to suffer by deciding what we "deserve."

As tribes grew into larger gatherings and settled into crystallized cultures with their own religions, rituals and pronounced way of life, they began to feel the urge to bend others to their realities. It was much safer to have no dissenting voices that could threaten the structures they had created or perhaps, anger their gods. Whether it was conquering lands or pitting gods against each other, religious wars began almost as early as the religions themselves. Great spans of time were swallowed up in these episodes of conquering and converting.

Religious believers were often martyred for their faith—whether they were Christians, Jews, Muslims, or others. Bringing in a new belief system about God always brought with it the possibility of death. They died because they found something bigger than themselves that conferred upon them a sense of goodness, piousness, and truth—something that made existence meaningful. We are still searching for that meaning—and all the suffering and martyrdom has not brought it to us.

If a new pharaoh, king, or governor chose a particular faith, all those under his rule were expected to immediately follow his lead. In effect, most of those followers had little else but God to belong to. There was no place to hide and no way of escaping the forceful fray of religious domination.

Imagine being a peasant at that time. There was virtually no sense of self, certainly no expression of personal power, and absolutely no education as to what it was all about. If you didn't hear about the switch of religious fidelity and quickly find a way to demonstrate your loyalty, you would become the victim of a violent takeover. There was a good chance you and your family would be destroyed anyway just for being there. The intricacies of religious protocol were very confusing then, as they are now.

Many who have been asked, or forced, to give up their lives for religious pretext are given some form of compensation, as in the old days when they were assured of God's grace. Suicide bombers are almost always promised some big reward for their families. Again, we see the shadowland between what is supposed to be for God, and what is, in fact, a political or cultural issue. Where there is the necessity of a bribe, no matter how nobly it is presented, there is an untruth that needs covering so that the seduction is sweetened by something other than the act itself.

Life was cruel in those times. I doubt we could withstand that level of suffering today. Physical pain was an accepted part of life, but it still was felt with all the same shock and hurt our bodies would record today. It is almost overwhelming to contemplate individual and collective experiences of such magnitude.

Let yourself imagine the feeling of being sacrificed—the moment of having your heart cut out, the push into a volcano or cenote. Imagine the conflict between the body and the mind in the act of self-torture as a part of atonement or purification—for God. These experiences are lurking within your cellular memories and triggering negative associations, even today.

The various inquisitions that overlapped the Crusades and bridged the witch hunts lasted almost 500 years! As early as 1184, at the Council of Verona, procedures for uncovering "heretics" were established. Finding heretics, seizing their land and belongings was such a successful way to get rid of people and frighten whole communities into submission that within fifty years, the "church" actually institutionalized the process by establishing "The Office of The Inquisition." In so doing, it officially gave power to certain individuals to ferret out suspicious individuals who might be a threat to the church because of their pagan activities, or knowledge of nature, or even something so frivolous as the look on their face. The power to seize property proved to be a gigantic motive for heretical accusation.

In Spain, the smear of a heretic could be levied for such offences as smiling at the mention of the Virgin Mary or eating meat on a day of abstinence. The accused were encouraged to denounce others, and by so doing, caused huge chain reactions in which the majority of the villagers could come under scrutiny. In fact, so terrible was the fear of the inquisitors, whole towns denounced themselves and each other in the hopes of being spared torture and death.

In all probability, the majority of the victims of the inquisitions were women who used herbs for healing or helped each other during birth. Though monks were allowed to have such knowledge, women were considered dangerous who knew the basic essentials about plants or healing. There are documents describing simultaneous burnings of many hundred heretics at one time. One source states that a French inquisitor burned **800** women in one day! Other accounts claim even more. Apparently, this happened frequently. Public punishments of heretics were set on feast days or sacred celebrations to heighten the drama, with kings and bishops in attendance. Imagine the space and materials it took to burn 1,000 people at once. It would appear that an entire valley had been set on fire.

The smell and sounds of humans being burned at the stake must have caused absolute chaos. Even the Knights Templar, who had served the Pope in the Crusades, were later burned alive as traitors when the mantle of power changed hands. No one was safe. As the church gained power over the monarchs, even the hierarchy, including men of the cloth, were mortified by the inquisitors. More than **5 million** people were burned at the stake, tortured or slaughtered in the name of God during these dark times.

Stop! Don't just read this. If you focused on it, you could probably still sense the unrelenting fear of being accused by an inquisitor of some amorphous wrongdoing.

Can you perceive the difference between simply bleeding, and that of blood spilling from wounds inflicted by the personification of the God Force? There is a difference. The body understands bleeding, but if that blood is produced through the phenomenal fear and emotional energetics of sacrifice or punishment, there is a heightened sensitivity wherein your seventy senses of perception will react as if you had been tortured in every aspect of your being, not just the physical!

We are **all** psychogenetically carrying these indelible impressions implanted collectively through the experiences of our forefathers and our own incarnations. Our genetic pool is so small that no one on the planet is further away from you than your forty-fourth cousin. That means that though you see yourself as a certain race and culture, even those opposite from you have imprinted you genetically! You are the Black, the Red, the Yellow—the Jew, the Muslim, the Hindu. Whatever has or is happening to *them* is also happening to you. If you could experience the truth of this consciously, our world would change abruptly. If the victimizer could feel the blight of the victim, victimization would stop.

You may think the holy wars are far removed from you, but they are just a flicker away from repeating themselves in the lives of your children's children. The equations will change and the downtrodden of today will become the perpetrators of tomorrow. Justified violence in the name of God is an addiction that is deeply entrenched in the human psyche. Religions still presume ownership over the lives of their adherents, whether it is in the form of social loyalty, financial commitment—or even the sacrifice of death.

Perhaps that is why God and violence seem to be so closely connected and why we are enthralled by violent books and movies today. Life, and especially death, brings us into this ancient conversation about God. Our primordial body longs to come out of the numbness of our lives and return to the thrill of constant danger, where it might again, "meet its Maker"—only because it remembers— and we have not been introduced to the vibrations of ecstasy, rapture and bliss that could carry us upward.

Early religious fervor spawned the dragon of self-righteousness that has so marred our religions today. The sense of smug superiority and complacency that comes from religious acts and affiliation has become the most common negative repertoire between religious groups of our time. In those early eras, it was justification for eradication of enemies, while at the present it is deeply attached to the Judeo-Christic ethic of judgment whereby everything and everyone is screened for defective qualities. Each church competes with a vengeance against all others to be exclusively correct in all conversations connected to God. Self-righteousness is in reality a defense mechanism to protect oneself from judgment by making the others seem less than the self. As with martyrdom, we have extracted the essence of self-righteousness and injected it into our daily lives as a buffer to our feelings of unworthiness.

There is a wealth of noble templates for martyrdom that lull us into the club of "good guys." Think of John the Baptist, Jesus the Christ, Joan of Arc, the saints or a thousand Tibetan monks. Political and social martyrs are abundant as well— Gandhi, Lincoln, Martin Luther King, the Kennedeys, Che Guevara and an infinite number of women and children worldwide. We need a new crop of human heroes who have not had to cast their lives into the dungeon of death to be remembered or honored.

All of these epics of religious evolution are a blur of time and places, but ultimately they swirl and mix together in a void of a forgotten past. It is hard for us to relate to them in the same way we cannot relate to the dimness of the cavemen, but they are part of who we are—the conquerors and the vanquished, the holy and the infidels, the martyrs and the priests.

In the end, we can understand how we came to see God the way we do, but if that becomes a pretext for our actions today, then the pretext becomes an excuse. Excuses always lead us away from truth and into the shadowy place where we feel justified to continue the very actions and beliefs that need changing. Lives lived under pretexts are unfulfilled lives of confusion, bound by the mind and entrapped by illusions of ancestry.

EVOLUTION

1. Let us separate sacrifice from offerings; offerings of our love, our devotion, our joy.

2. Let us clear the psychogenetic residues of spying, suspicion, accusing others for our own benefit.

THREE

THE CRUSADES:
RELIGION ON THE MOVE

*The Crusades, and all "holy wars," are a travesty
against humanity and the sacredness of life!*

WHILE MY HEART WANTS TO RUSH AHEAD to the hopeful and inspirational possibilities of the evolution of God, my mind holds me in its iron vise and insists, "Finish it." It is pushing me to go deeper into these dark sleeves of our history wherein we lived literally by the sword of God. This is not only true of the last two thousand years of religion, but holy war was prevalent long before the time of Christ and the glorified sword of God was used during the ancient epics of Africa, Egypt, India and all of Asia.

I remember the songs I heard as a child that were sung with such conviction, "… Onward Christian soldiers, onward as to war…." How cleverly were the threads of righteousness sown into the cloth of religious belief. We must march forward and slay anything or anyone foreign to our god. That song somehow weaves the deeds of the Crusades into a fabric of religious approval and even justification. God wanted us to superimpose the ways of our religion onto the lives of all others—at the peril of death.

The Crusades have become an indelible stain on the cloak of spiritual endeavor. Even kings, bound by the fearsome power of

God's representatives, saw the wisdom of bending non-believers to the will of their god and extolling not only their allegiance, but their wealth, lands and identity—along the way.

Of course the initial Crusades found justification in the emotionally gripping campaign to regain the holy city of Jerusalem, which was held sacred to the triad of religions—Jews, Christians and Muslims. Imagine the power of Pope Urban II inciting the Christian world with his words, "Christ commands it!" What a travesty to even imply that the great model of gentleness, love and peace would command war as a method of spreading his teachings. No, this Crusade was not an edict from above, but rather a misguided effort issued from below, to regain a place of religious reverence that, in actuality, could have been shared with the Muslims and the Jews who also held it sacred. Instead, Jews were brutalized for killing Christ and the streets of Jerusalem ran thick with everyone's blood.

Would that the Pope's efforts had been focused on the power of love and peace that cannot (ever) be misplaced or taken away by the illusory ownership of land. Perhaps the focus on a "place" of sacredness as essential to the worship of God, rather than an experience of presence, began there!

Politics and God have always been intertwined in the visions of the few and the submission of the many! Crusading in God's name, however heart-felt by the knights who carried out the deeds, was inevitability a perfect opportunity for "the powers that be" to rid themselves of enemies, opponents, and obstacles that stood in their way. Properties were stolen, lives were taken, and powers were usurped. When a battle was won, the losers were mercilessly slaughtered in blood baths that still darken the hearts of all humanity.

The Crusades were a medieval media initiative. By religiously flaunting the powerful symbol of the cross and its story of the crucifixion, they were able to self-righteously justify the slaughter, the witch burning, and torture they imposed upon the innocents who had no choice but to subscribe to the frenzied format of Christian faith—or die terrible deaths. It will probably never be recognized that untold helpless people fell to this unyielding force, merely as pawns in the show of power. Their lives had no value other than to impress upon the masses the expediency of survival through submission. In the fray of the later Crusades, even knights were burned at the stake as heretics.

Let us not elude ourselves that some nobility was attached to the Crusades—no matter what is written in the history books. The Crusades were not the mandate of the God Force, they were plotted and carried out by the hand of man—a hand that reached out to grab land and spoils of war equally as fervently as to defend faith. The church—in fact, all churches—must ultimately take responsibility for the slanderous and manipulative presentation of "God's will!" And what is the sixth commandment brought by Moses in the 13th century B.C.E.? "Thou shall not kill!" Did the god of those tortuous times forget to attach the disclaimer—only in his name? No, even the gods can fall prey to the will of man!

We humans still qualify those commandments to suit our realities; and God has always been the great pretext of justification for otherwise most grievous doings. We have not laid down the crutch of "justifiable killing." War seems as inevitable and profitable today as it was then—we have not yet passed on to the initiation of peace.

That self-righteousness of spirit that drove knights to murder in the name of God has become a template for religious victory through "God by force." The ignoble deeds of the Crusaders were yet another ripple of that aggressive yang perspective in which man thinks he has the right to force his will on others. The Crusades, and all "holy wars," are a travesty against humanity and the sacredness of life!

Equally as treacherous as the Crusades have been the various holy wars mounted by Islam, a religion that espouses peace and continues to offer up war to the world. Like the Christians, the Muslims have fought amongst themselves over power since the very beginning of their religion. The blood spilled from these repetitious events is still hardening the hearts of the various sects that hold the battles of their ancestors insipidly in their veins. Orthodox and non-orthodox Christians, Shi'ites and Sunni Muslims alike, took their turns assaulting each other for reasons that may have seemed valid to them, but which are unjustifiable in light of the commandments brought by Moses that all claim to respect; to say nothing of our sense of humanity today.

True, it was a time of crude violence that fit the realities of those ages, and we must see it as a part of a spiraling evolution from which we would like to claim ourselves immune. Yet, how can we? We are still engaging in our own modern versions of Crusades. The link between God and righteous struggle is so entrenched in our psyche that it is difficult to imagine that we can see past the superfluous banners of its pretense into the darkened spaces of its secret intent.

I am sure that our page in history will also report our deeds of global interference and control as something less than optimal humanitarianism. The slaughter of the First Americans by priests and soldiers of the cross, the quiet induction of Hawaiians into the Protestant faith, Israel's battles over the Promised Land with Palestine, the violent attacks of jihad are all the righteous veneers of religious politics in their most insidious extreme.

Today, though we might not condone witch hunting in the physical, or so blatantly misuse the club of religion to instigate our goals, we do still wield that club at the heads of all others whom we deem a threat to our place as the favorites of God. That illusionary status is our justification for the embattlements in which we engage—politically and otherwise. "God is on our side," is the refrain of all such clashes—and ironically, it is intoned on both sides of the battlefield.

The Pope and Muhammad both exhorted their men into battle by these very sentiments, and when they won, expounded on how God rewarded the faithful. When they lost, that ploy did not hold up—whereby, the soldiers were immediately castigated for their impurity, lack of faith or passion to die for God. Why do the pawns not recognize themselves? Because it is in their nature to submit to more powerful forces without ever wondering if there is something beyond servitude.

Along with the belief of favoritism has come the threat of God's vengeance upon those who do not please or obey. As in the earliest of times, misfortune has been interpreted as the hand of God. Virtually every major religion has some concept about how God will punish you—or the others—for not doing his bidding. Vengeance has always been the most honored and condoned action by religious fundamentalists who project it onto their God.

What is this desperation to be "first" in the eyes of God? I think it is the primordial residue of favoritism that once insured survival. If you were not within the fold, you were in danger of a kind of expulsion that was equivocal to death, if not death itself. There seems to be no time shield that could protect us from these old whisperings that were not only fabricated in distant times, but are every bit the same destructive props of today.

Religious fanatics on all sides are still re-enacting those precise patterns and poisoning our future. How could the Irish Catholics and Protestants pretend that killing each other in the name of God holds any justification? It might be about religion, social dominance, or cultural positioning, but it is NOT about God! How convenient to brand it into the psyche of the faithful and then feed it as a diet of hatred that becomes an unfathomable addiction, inherited by future generations!

Religious domination must become a thing of the past if we are to catch the next rung of the ladder and evolve as a species. In the United States, the Founding Fathers attempted to separate church and state in order to avoid the pitfalls that resulted from their union in the countries the immigrants had escaped. Witness the resurgence of religious power that has re-entered the political arena here today. Its lobbyists eternally rant about what God-fearing people must do in order to be within the fold.

It is dangerous to allow such fanatical tirades to bully the masses into choices they might not make, except for the fear of God's wrath perpetually held over their heads. It is time for us to collectively—grow up! We are not the quivering children we were thousands of years ago. We can use the clarity of our consciousness to see for ourselves what is true and what is merely a mask of persuasion.

The fanatics of all religions will continue to desperately cling to their place on the ladder because fanaticism is based on an all-encompassing rigidity that does not compromise with variation or separate reality. There are no choices, no conciliation, only the desperate struggle to be right. In the encapsulated world of the fanatic, it is the "presumed" word of God that comforts and buries the hurt of being ostracized by assuring them that they are the righteous, the "chosen" ones.

In effect, each religious group feels it is the chosen, and through that insidious link to selfhood, they trade freedom for the yoke of submission and the offering of sacrifice to a God force that indubitably never asked for it.

Though the present Islamic "holy wars" are partly a subversive defense mechanism for a people who have suffered the indignation of disrespect and misunderstanding, they are still deadly weapons wielded at the world under the un-impenetrable guise of religious righteousness. The bloody Crusades against the Muslims have not been wrenched from their psychogenetic repertoire, and for a frighteningly growing segment of Islamic fanatics, this will not be amended until Muslims find satisfaction in their own form of vengeance—thus perpetuating the unending battle. Now it is the Christians, Jews and all others who have become the infidels, the unholy, the unworthy—the same words levied at the Muslims during the Crusades. The Muslims must, however, take responsibility for the fact that they, too, unleashed their swords against others who did not embrace their religious truths—including other Islamic sects!

There are no victims here within these religious massacres, because none are free from the blight of religious wars they themselves have instigated. The victimizers pounce upon those they can override, who await their moment to payback the injustice with even greater vengeance. The cycle of dominance and destruction has passed hands from one to another, and another, down to the present day without any appreciable lull in the campaigns for power.

It is much easier to enlist warriors into the battle if you implore them with "God wills it so!" Every religion has its own version of this powerful refrain of manipulation. It can be used to prod the hesitant—into war, into submission, into justification. Again, it is a select few who command the lives of millions—painting the canvas of their reality with hatred and fear. Attaching the insult to our god as a motive for war is an easy sell to those who need something bigger to belong to and fight for. God has historically been the pretext of justification for killing and may continue to be, unless we evolve from the concept of—

"My God against your God."

In the case of Judaism, Christianity, and Islam the absurdity is that, in essence, they share the same God, the same fundamental messages and even the same sacred soil. Only their different cultures sculpt God into an image that they each can call their own. All three religions are built on supposed directives from God as to how to live life. How unfortunate that we have not yet learned to live those mandates, but perpetually twist them into arguable discourses of interpretation and execution.

All the descriptions of God, thus far, contain the taint of human projection. We have assigned our own motives, characteristics, and dubious proclamations onto our god. Is it any wonder that we refuse to allow changes in our creation? Time, as we know it, *does* change truth! It is inextricably entwined with the wisdom of experience. Life exposes and illuminates truth. Yet, we stubbornly refuse to allow ourselves to see The Divine in new ways. The consequences of that denial have been profoundly detrimental to our evolution.

Why do we linger with the god of the Crusaders, the god of the Israelites, Allah, or any of these violent ones who presumably demand war and death against the non-believers? No true god who has the power to create universes would ask these things. Can't we see that this war mongering is only the twisted mind of MAN? It is not done for "the glory of God," it is a thinly disguised bid for ultimate power. What lethal fog is this to think that God would be glorified by destroying Divine creation? We are only being exposed to a shadow form of The Divine—a filter clogged by the density of human thought and deed.

We are so entrenched in these religious imprints that they will be exceedingly difficult to release, because our very cultures are embedded in them. The bloody memories of our forefathers have become the insidious spores of mold that lurk within our own blood. We are repeating the Crusades, the jihad, the holy wars now, under different pretexts, but the energy and, in fact, the goals are the same.

Nations around the world are sending troops into the Middle East to fight for...what? For forgotten oaths of vengeance and dominance? For fear of nuclear advantage? For oil and secret booty? The justifications are endless and the guises complete, but the outcome will be the same—a treadmill of unwinnable skirmishes and an impassable trench of death.

I know that there seemed no other choice in those ages of darkness except to do what they knew to do. Kill or be killed, was a constant of war—but the slaughter of innocents was, and is, a terrible fester that we all must heal—from within. The commandment of "thou shall not kill" was placed within reach of human consciousness millenniums before it could ever be recognized as a prerequisite for a higher octave of living. Today, we use that edict for our domestic laws, but it is lost in the collective fortresses of war, which gives sanctuary to mass killing of human beings.

I am not interested in blame or justification, or theological arguments, I am only interested in moving on to a better world in which we can live without fear of our god or anyone else's. Hopefully, I am shining the light on a passage of our human/God relationship that needs to come to an end—through our enlightened awareness of it—not our defensive stances as to who was to blame, or whether it was justifiable.

One thing is true: all religions have attempted to increase their girth by engaging in the gamut of persuasive tactics from threat and death, to seduction through booty and God's grace. Can you imagine a Pope selling favors in heaven in exchange for going on a Crusade? Pope Urban II did just that. He promised absolution for all sins committed on the Crusade, plus booty, plus passage to heaven in order to entice men into the campaign. This is not infallibility; this is blatant misuse of power in God's name!

After all these thousands of years, we are still fighting and killing. What will it take to tear ourselves away from the lure of power, the spoils of war, the dominance of physical force, the oppression of authority? We don't need to fight over God—look what it has brought us! History is repeating itself. If we do not find a new way to relate to the Divine Source, we will elongate this passage—into infinity.

We fight about God because we do not feel that we can touch The Divine except through books, rituals, or structure. Yet each and all of us suffer, because that Divine energy is buried within our own spiritual DNA. We have an incomprehensible and mysterious sense of it, but we cannot find a way to access it. We must give ourselves permission to embody Divine energy. To do that, we will have to strengthen our inner sense of The Divine and find our own direct spiritual link to God through a new kind of oneness. We are not programmed for spiritual autonomy and no organized religious institution will allow this—we will have to choose it for ourselves. I am not saying we must disavow our churches; I am saying we can reconstruct them and create new ones. The crux of the problem is that we do not yet know we want this kind of power and freedom.

Does it seem to you that there is no way out of this dilemma because it is so intertwined with the convoluted nature of humans? There is a way out. In fact, there are many ways out, but none of them will take place until we have the courage to call them forward. We must dissolve our fear of dissention and the sanctimonies of the churches, so we can discard all remnants of our dishonest religious past.

There are many religious residues from the time of the Crusades that are choking the throat of spiritual evolution. As we clear them from our psychogenetic repertoire, the breathless beauty of peace will appear as a beacon on the horizon and we will all hear its call.

I have contemplated several thoughtforms from the Crusades that I think are indispensable to **release** so that we are no longer caught in the blind spots of their conclusions.

What would you add to this list?

- Crusades and holy wars were necessary and noble.
- Religious war is for the glory of God.
- We must fight—"my god against your god."
- God is on our side.
- God will reward fighting in his name.

(Please see Chapter 12, *Technology of Consciousness*—releasing thoughtforms.)

I truly see no other way out of the territorial embattlements of religions without a new element of Divine perspective—The Evolution of God.

EVOLUTION

1. Let us embrace the joy that we humans share in the consciousness of divinity.

2. Clear all residues of the Crusades and any associations as to their nobility from your body. (See Chapter 12, *Technology of Consciousness.*)

3. Clear any psychogenetic residues of fighting for God from your body. (See Chapter 12, *Technology of Consciousness.*)

FOUR

THE CROSS

LIFE IS A QUEST TO IDENTIFY TRUTH and the self. We use all manner of markings to show the world who we are, especially to convince ourselves that we exist and belong, because that sense of identity is what makes us feel safe. In times of fearful reality, we turn to anything that gives us an easy prescription to follow for life, and we surround ourselves in all its trappings. Read the messages on T-shirts, designer logos across the pockets of shirts and jackets, the images chosen for body tattoos and you can see the labels of an aspiring self. Our jewelry and clothes in general convey the messages we wish to present to the world.

Religions, likewise, use icons and symbols to imprint a lasting image of their beliefs and points of identification. The cross is an excellent example of this. Its history as an esoteric and religious symbol long predates Christianity, and its actual form has been given many variations—some ornate, some absolute simplicity. The cross appears on rugs and clothing, alters and art from millennia before the impingement of Christianity. It existed in classical Egypt and other early cultures as an object of power and authority. Egyptian priests and kings carried the Egyptian ankh cross form as a symbol of life and authority related to the god of the sun. The Native Americans used the equal cross to signify the crossroads, the intersection of energies as a point of power.

The swastika cross form was used by Mesopotamians, Taoists, Tibetans, the Maya, Navajo, and others from as early as 1000 B.C.E. Adolf Hitler forever destroyed its benign symbol of luck and goodness, and it is doubtful that its association with the power of destruction will ever be diminished.

The Christian cross is possibly the most powerful of religious icons and its reference point of suffering has become a kind of pre-requisite for godliness. It carries with it a multitude of messages about the concept of suffering, original sin, and Christ as savior to humankind. The "Jesus on the cross" theme of Christiandom is used to remind Christians that Christ died for our sins, and if we remember that, it could help us to be better Christians. I can understand why the thought of Jesus on the cross could help early Christians withstand their own dying for their faith. The symbol of the cross may have helped them to feel brave—to suffer well. If Jesus could do it, so could they. But the crucifix was not actually used as the church standard until around the 6th century C.E., and not until the 10th century does his suffering image on the cross appear. Perhaps it was because Jewish tradition did not allow any visual representation of God in the physical form, and even though Jesus was a disputed manifestation of the prophesy, it was not expedient to replay the scene.

The first Christian icon was the fish, a message of life, not death. However, by 160 C.E., people began to make the sign of the cross on their foreheads to signify "the sign of the lord." Later, in times of persecution, the quick drawing of the cross on the body was a code for secret Christian identification. Today it most represents the message of the Holy Trinity—Father, Son and Holy Gost, and is often used as a gesture of self-protection.

The real dilemma of the crucifix comes back to the belief in original sin. Implicit in the message of the cross is that we are implicated in Jesus' death and suffering simply because we exist, because we have inherited the "sins" of Adam and Eve. How could this be? We were not there; we did not do it. The concept of being born sinners because of any ancestral link simply does not satisfy rational truth. The Catholic church is still discussing whether newborn babies who have not been baptized will languish in hell for eternity or not! Such scare tactics have no justification and are unworthy of Christian tenants.

Any guilt for such a heinous act as crucifixion belongs to our forefathers and their own foul justification for political and religious injustice. Why would we be guilty for the choices of two thousand years ago? This concept is a carry-over from ancient cultures that has held us ransom for the actions of our elders. The time span then did not correlate to thousands of years; it spoke to generational realities. It is past time to release it.

The story that God sent "his only begotten son to die for our sins" smacks of the strict and negative manipulative tactics of ancient times. Most of religion began with that thrust whereby the angry god needed to be pacified through our repentance, rather than the more enlightened perspective that we were given Divine examples of how to express life in terms of our profound and loving relationship with God. That inspiring possibility would have had a completely different outcome of spiritual awakening, and could have guided all humanity through a breathtaking funnel of initiation to an enlightened world. Unfortunately, our ancestors had no such repertoire within the reality of their life, and so the human filter could not allow such energies to be seeded into our spiritual DNA.

However, crucifixion did not end the teachings of Jesus. The attempt to get rid of a political troublemaker failed. It is even plausible to conclude that the great healer, Jesus the Christ, did not actually perish on that cross. There was no conclusive death on the cross, no body—just an empty tomb. How the stone was rolled away, and by whom, is a mystical story in itself.

A rising pitch of controversy about the final result of Jesus' crucifixion is beginning to rage across the world as a growing number of researchers and seekers are exploring the viable possibility that Jesus lived on. This does not preclude his resurrection or ascension, because they are inherent in transcending from one physical level to a higher level of "light body" existence. Nor does it rule out the possibility that he moved back and forth from physical to ethereal states after his crucifixion. These are the mysteries that give Jesus the right of Divine example and the authority of spiritual teachings. They are what make his life important to us, not the mundane story of his suffering. This pitiful boast of fame is entirely unworthy of the master he was, and the church's emphasis on the crucifixion instead of the resurrection has become a great injustice to human evolution.

It is recorded that many masters were able to bilocate, astral-project and otherwise appear and disappear at will. During the years Jesus was occulted from history, it may be that he was, as some researchers claim, cloistered in the apprenticeship of such advanced beings. Since he apparently learned the laws of undoing death, we may assume that he also knew these other forms of energy mastery. He showed them to his followers as a template of Divine life, but higher laws were too far advanced for their limited consciousness in the same way that we still pretend them unrelated to our own abilities.

If we are an evolving species of Divine origin, then we need not carry with us into the future the limited concepts and conclusions of the constrictive past. What we do need to embrace is the power of love, the gift of healing and the mystery of eternal life. All of these were demonstrated by Jesus and others within the scope of their lifetimes. Isn't that why their names and stories have been passed down through the ages?

The theory of the cross was that Christ suffered and died to save us. How could salvation be the purpose of our lives? That would imply a fallacy of Divine intent to have created imperfect life that ran amuck on its own. Evolution itself is a guideline for improvement, not punishment. Salvation is a concept bred of fear and intertwined with pain. A civilization that uses the glue of suffering and death to bind it can only bring forth that kind of world.

Why would we be put into body just to be saved? No, we are here for a much more enlightened destiny. We have come to evolve and carry back to our Divine Source the fruit of our quest so that all manifest life could be enhanced by our infinite potential. Today, we should be throwing off the shackles of martyrdom and embodying the teachings of the life and miracles that Christ gave to us.

Let us leap off this rung of the ladder wherein spiritual truth is eclipsed by the expediency of politics and power—as is still true today! We have spent almost 2000 years focusing on the cross of Christendom, and its power as an icon has all but destroyed the teachings of Jesus the Christ. The very fact that Christian churches have put the crucifixion foremost into the consciousness of their followers, lays bare the question of some profound imbalance—if not covert manipulation.

Do our religious leaders think that the sight of Jesus on the cross is the most important revelation of Christianity? Tens of thousands of people were crucified at the time of Christ. The crucifixion of Jesus is not in itself outstanding. Much more unimaginable is his own motive. Why did he do it? It could not be about treachery or victimization. It was a choice he made whose meaning we cannot surmise from the consciousness of below. The Gospel of Judas states that Jesus asked him to set the plan—why? It was not for death's sake alone. He intended something beyond it. Perhaps we are only now about to conceive of his true intention. Certainly, he expected more of us; perceived us to be more advanced than we were—or even are now!

It never made sense to me that a great being who could raise the dead and heal the sick would simply suffer and die on the cross. It is unfathomable that such a master of physical law could have been the victim, or chose to exemplify the contradiction of helplessness. What would have been the purpose? We have never really allowed ourselves to pierce the veil of martyrdom in order to ask such a question. I am certain that it had to do with opening the veil onto an expanded horizon of cosmic truth.

Christ gave us a fleeting human glimpse at the existence of another most magnificent octave, whereby all sorrow and loss could be erased and life itself could be reclaimed. He was doing something that our forefathers simply could not cognate. He showed us the truth of the body. He showed us transcendence, but he did it in such a convoluted way that we missed the message. We imprinted suffering and death, rather than transmutation and higher consciousness!

What is worthy of inspiration is that he may have transmuted crucifixion as a teaching about the body—resurrection, transcendence, and ascension. Why is it that so little merit is paid to his resurrection? It is acknowledged, but nothing in depth is taught about this greatest miracle of all. Perhaps it is because Jesus' own disciples (with the exception of Mary Magdalene) could not comprehend it or anchor it into the tenets of Christian theology.

The ornate and beautiful crosses of the Orthodox Greek Church do not utilize the Christ figure suffering on them. The Orthodox chose to see the purity of Christ's mission to teach resurrection and transcendence. They saw the cross as the vehicle Jesus used to demonstrate that we could defeat death. Their approach seems much more aligned to the Christed intention.

Jesus asked us to copy his miracles, and yet multitudes who have even performed such small reflections as healing have met with punishment or death at the hands of his own church for such a supposed transgression as to pretend likeness to him.

Christian doctrine has not as yet given ascendance to us to embrace as a joyful and pivotal spiritual truth. Instead, it has fixated on the gory death of a godly figure, overshadowing an exemplar life of human dignity and love, with pain and sorrow. We have tethered ourselves to a negative version of aspiring to be godlike and placed the cloak of guilt around our burdened shoulders.

Once, at the Vatican in Rome, I overheard this conversation between a mother and her young son. They were standing reverently before a large statue of Jesus on the cross. The sword wound, the nails in the hands, the blood dripping from the crown of thorns, and the saddest tear from Jesus' eye vividly displayed all the tragic details. I watched the small boy taking in each one with a mixture of awe and horror.

His mother whispered to him, "Look sweetheart, here is Jesus on the cross."
The boy looked up at his mother in shock and said, "But why is he on the cross, Mommy?"
"Because he died for your sins."
"What sins, Mommy?"
"For being born."
"Oh," he sighed dejectedly and hung his head.

It is unspeakable to contemplate that this little boy will carry such a negative, guilty nuance of himself throughout life and that such a core imprint will not be erased, even if one day he realizes that he is not responsible for what happened to Jesus. It will lurk beneath the surface of his consciousness fomenting a vague sense of unnamed guilt. His true self will drown in this undercurrent, and he will unlikely become a Christed being because he will never know that he is worthy of it.

It was all I could do to not rush over and attempt to neutralize this terrible poison being thrust on him, but of course, I had no right to interfere. May all the mothers of the world hear this story and free their children from its terrible grip! The stories of Christ's miracles are lost in the images of the crucifix and the overwhelming message that even saviors are victims!

What do you feel when you see a crucifix? I am sure that you do not smile or feel ecstatic? It would be a sacrilege to not at least offer the sentiment of pain and guilt in the face of this potent message–that Jesus died for your sins. But did he? It is possible that the entire episode has another meaning. I do not feel that spiritually anyone outside the self (one's own Soul) can take away the inevitable fact of another's actions/sins. If that were possible, then the great being, Jesus the Christ, who raised the dead, would have no need for destroying his own sacred life to save ours! He could have dissolved our karma in the same way he took away sickness.

We will not fully go on from this gruesome epic of human development until we have come to terms with the basic tenant that humanity is so bad that we cannot be worthy of higher realms. If we took the crucifixion out of the equation between Christ and ourselves, we might truly begin to claim our inheritance as the heirs of mystical gifts that have been exemplified, offered and passed to us by Christ himself! Jesus gave us not only permission, but a mandate, as well. Organized religion may never risk such a magnanimous gesture as to encourage that kind of autonomy—we will have to claim it ourselves!

One way to begin that inheritance of miraculous life is to review all the representations of religious faith and remove those, such as the crucifixion, that hold us to fearful and un-enlightened expression. We can create beautiful icons that lift us to new heights of spiritual inspiration. The Christ on the mountain that looks over the city of Rio de Janeiro is one of my favorite examples. It is a statue of Jesus with his arms flung open as if to embrace everyone and everything.

Religions have amplified the perspective of good and evil—of polarity and separation. If our vision and comprehension were expanded enough, we would see that the polarities always join and part and join and part like the double helix spiral of evolution. Perhaps completing the embracing arms of Christ on the mountain in Brazil would bring us back to the circle, which is an eternal symbol used from the dawn of time to speak the language of oneness.

Christian churches must rid their walls of the image of Jesus on the cross if they are to continue into the future as focal points of Christ's teaching. Suffering is not Divine! The inhumane acts we see in our world today are sourced in those terrible archaic imprints perpetrated by religious misunderstanding. They do not belong in human repertoire. It is truly unworthy of Jesus' message and his life. He taught love, not violence. He taught the power of miracles, not subjugation of the body. If the focus of Christian doctrine had not been on crucifixion, we might be already accomplishing the transmutation of death! If we are going to evolve our spiritual faculties, we must shift the visual and emotional symbology we attach to our sense of religious truth so we can evolve new spiritual realities and become, ourselves, Christed.

If we remove the crucifixion as a pivotal part of Christianity, we could make Easter the sacred celebration of life that it should be. The true meaning of Easter began in pagan times when a new cycle of life was celebrated each spring. What if Easter were not about death on the cross, but rather the miracle of life and transcendence from lower to higher realms of consciousness! In keeping with our morbid view that we cannot arrive at the goal without sufficient suffering, the breathtaking realization of transfiguration has been plastered over. Christians feel so profoundly the thought of this man suffering on the cross, but in effect, if we can not extend that sorrow to all the other tens of thousands of people who died on the cross of inhumanity, or the sons and daughters who are dying today in the wars of political or religious illusion, then there is an untruth to the gesture of our righteous pain.

The only viable future of Christian churches is the discovery of Jesus' physical and spiritual mastery and how to perform miracles ourselves. Transmutation of the body and the laws of ascension are the true legacies offered to all of humanity through the crucifixion of Jesus the Christ. Christian priests and ministers have not offered them to us because they have not learned them themselves. Why? Perhaps because they have held their attention on mental faculties rather than the energetic teachings given by Christ. They could learn them, and so could we, if only we allowed ourselves to lift up into the frequencies Jesus used to perform his miracles. A world without sickness, fear of death or hunger would be a world worthy of our true destiny.

Beyond the condemnation of the cross, we could begin to erase the judgment and blame that have been heaped upon the Jews since the Crusaders slaughtered them, exploiting the justification that it was their fault Jesus was crucified. How quickly they blurred the fact that these were his own people. Peace and compassion between the Jewish and Christian faiths is paramount to a new world and the removal of the crucifixion theme will help us to refocus our attention onto the beautiful example he set for us all.

EVOLUTION

1. Remove all images of Christ on the cross from churches, jewelry and other paraphernalia so that his great power is not degraded as a victim.

2. Christianity without the cross will revolutionize its religion. Let us open our consciousness to new icons that better describe Christ.

3. Let us reconfigure Easter as a celebration of miracles and ascension.

4. Meditate on the resurrection of your body and ascension as a state of consciousness you can attain.

PART TWO

Today

FIVE

RELIGIOUS CONCEPTS

DESPITE THE TEACHINGS ON HOW TO LIVE LIFE given in the sacred texts of religious doctrine, religious concepts today are held hostage by the insistence on the un-changeability of the perspectives set forth by those teachings in a world very different than the present. Even for those who are certain that the messages were given directly from God, it is not a travesty to view them as a gift of time and place to the ones who so needed them in that historical era. To question all of life is our Divine right. In ancient times, only a few could stretch their awareness out from the struggle of daily life to seek something profound and related to them spiritually. However, the confines of their choices and awareness were too narrow and too incomplete to guide us now. We must open our consciousness and hearts to possible new Divine experiences.

Do we need to continue with only the cast of characters we had thousands of years ago? Are there still the Judases, the Judges, the martyrs and the prophets? It is sad to consider that on some levels we are still very much within their same repertoire of themes, even today: treachery, jealousy, illusion and the hunger for power. It is not infallibility or righteousness we need, it is not words of vengeance, or holy war or punishment. It is not the judgment as to who is the worthy or valuable or chosen one—all of those fearful and destructive imprints have left us in a pit of darkness without a ladder of ascension to bring us into a place free from danger, guilt and sorrow.

Certainly the deepest spiritual truths of compassion, love, and connection to The Divine are timeless treasures that will forever be a part of the human template, but it is time to allow ourselves to see them from the perspective of our own realities—without the label of blasphemy! We need not embrace them through suffering and martyrdom; our forefathers have already done that. We can best learn their offerings by practicing them in every moment of our lives.

Today, it is the mandate of our entire Soul group present on this planet to awaken, evolve and practice the meaning of "free will" given us by the Divine Source. Free will is the gift of choice through which we sculpt experience into destiny. It is our spiritual mandate to take responsibility for those choices that have led us to today. We have the power to create our own reality, to grow and evolve through our experiences and conscious awareness. It isn't that we can make everything the way we want it, but rather that we have the freedom to use all experience as a guideline of purpose to show us cause and effect, and therefore how to choose life. We can only do this if we open to higher spiritual energies and integrate them into our lives. It is awareness of our evolutionary potential and its amplification that awaits our unedited creative flow.

Our religious concepts are still entirely too limited to cover the issues and realities of our lives without some revision and expansion. Let us be brave enough to accomplish the necessary changes within the adventure of new discoveries. In the near future our children will travel to the moon, the bottom of the seas, out into the galaxy, and they will bring home new concepts about God that will shake the core of our present truths. Are we to stop them from that? Traditionalists and defendants of literal religious interpretation will not be able to denounce their discoveries and will be stranded on a beach of irrelevance in an outgoing tide. The future generations of explorers will add new pieces to the God puzzle that may show us how to be a part of something much bigger than we have imagined!

How can we lift up from the constrictive patterns of our ancestors and bring in a new kind of spirituality that advances our relationship to The Divine? What would it be like? First and foremost, we would be free of fear and guilt. We would allow ourselves to commune on the higher octaves of love, without judging our faults. Our themes would not be about worthiness, but ecstasy, rapture and bliss.

Will we make the leap from a homogeneous God to a universal Divine Source without losing our sense of self? What if the human form of God is nothing more than our own unique point of reference? Do the other sentient beings see God only in their own likeness? We are exceedingly limited by our dependence on recognizable form to make something real for us, yet we have not actually seen a self-professed god in human form. We have seen a reflection of Divine principles in a Buddha, a Christ, holy men and women, and others—but not God itself. We speak of the lord of the heavens, but we have not a glimmer as to what that really means.

The concept that humans were created in God's image is one of wishful context without any other confirmation than that the early religions said so. No one saw God. They saw angels and those like Jesus who were said to be of Him. I find this to be part of the very quaint human illusion that everything in the universe must be about us or like us. Of course, it is easier for humans to relate to God with the image of human form as the lord who governs our lives. It would be harder to follow the edicts of daily rule from a nebulous god form. Hopefully, as we evolve we will not need these edicts at all.

In the biblical creation story God says, "Let us make man in our image" (Genesis1:26). This opens up another seemingly unanswerable question—"Who is us?" Speaking in the plural implies that there was more than one creator or some form of collective consciousness that participated in our genesis. If we knew the answer to this enigma, we might be able to revise the entire basis of our god relationship!

At this point we seem certain that God must be in the masculine form because that has been the dominating force for the duration of human religious epics. However, if we believe that "he" made our species in his form, then he/she must be female as well, since we are half female genetically. If we think back to the primordial times when "might makes right" was in full effect and physical strength was the essential attribute, we can see why it was the males who were the chosen ones to negotiate with the violent and powerful god we saw in natural forces.

Do you think that if the first shamans and priests were female we would have conceived of human sacrifice? No, a woman would not throw away her creation, which she labored to bring into the world. Therefore, we must acknowledge that it was not God who demanded the destruction of the life, but rather it was man—who could not feel the power of birthing, that conceived of sacrifice. Again, why would a god be pleased by the killing of its own creation?

We have reported "god sightings" in the form of a burning bush as well as the voice of God through an angel, and we accepted these as true. Sound and light are worthy godly energies and perhaps it is time to open up to other Divine communiqués that broaden our repertoire in terms of the form of God. Religions rely on very focused representations of the god form to lend authority to their doctrine. It is much easier to accept the dictates of a god who might speak to us as a father than some unknowable, invisible power. But the Divine essence actually permeates every conscious choice to touch God, beyond the props of our senses or the format of religious design.

Our spiritual DNA confers upon us the knowing of God's essence as the center point of our very being, and is therefore always within our power to access it. If we are created by God, then we must hold some part of that God force within us. We cannot be wrenched from God by any externalized judgment or wrongdoing, because The Divine is the essence of being-ness, not the doing.

Most religions today still use a maze of doctrine, rules and pre-scribed rituals to guide their constituents through the circuitous pathways to heaven, nirvana, or enlightened consciousness. They have rules that must be followed to extract God's approval. What to wear, eat, do—when to pray, how to please God through sacrifice, abstention or some other form of denial—are all orchestrated by human filters and presumptions based on a very humanized and even cultural version of the God Force.

The ways we integrate God into our lives could be considered our cultural treasures, but they are not any more or less true from a spiritual perspective; they are simply the form that fits our way of living. The symbolism we use and even our conceptual awareness are begotten by eras of human consciousness and should be revised as we evolve our truths. God did not say you should not expose your body or that you had to cover your head. The covering of the head is a left over from thousands of years of tradition. It is only a gesture, a thoughtform about what is respectful, pure, or holy, entrapped in a time capsule.

These traditional patterns may be honored because they are cultural values, but they are only virtual truth and must not be confused with deeper spiritual laws. It is a terrible travesty that they inflict so much suffering—especially to women. Perhaps as we evolve, we will "choose" our cultural expressions rather than be punished by non-compliance to them.

We continue with our religions not so much because we do not see the fallacies, incongruities and even deceptions, but because we need the sense of belonging, the comfort of habit, and the continuity of our cultures. Is that enough? For an increasing number of people, the answer is no. It is certainly possible that some of our religious loyalty is more about our cultural roots than about God. It is the holidays we celebrate, the rituals that have translated God into our lives that are crucial to us, and therefore we need to distinguish between cultural and spiritual realities.

Many people have expressed that their fear is not about what would happen to their religion, but what would happen to their place in society that causes them the hesitancy of changing how they express their religious faith. Religion, per se, may continue into the future not so much because we believe in the specific dogma of a church, but because we could not do without the marking of passages such as marriage, baptism, confirmation, and funerals that are entrenched in our collective societal functions. In these moments we feel the need to have some higher authority link us to the God Force and each other. We need a kind of formality to officiate these gatherings and it will take time and practice to see how we can create new ceremonies of passage under our own volition. We still search for leaders who have "studied" God; and through their mastery of intellectual innuendos and historic guideposts, are therefore capable of rendering the mystical into our waiting minds.

We have yet to comprehend that The Divine is not a depository of the rational, but the energetic key to our essence. The leap of spiritual autonomy, while on the horizon, is a far distance from our present reality. We would have to stretch up to a new octave of consciousness to become one with the Divine Source without an interpreter.

That level would necessitate a fusion of mind and heart wherein awareness could include the input of higher emotions and feeling. Our spiritual pain has been born squarely on the shoulders of our emotional and mind bodies. I am sure that our collective emotional bodies have not embraced a god that does not inspire fear, because fear is so insidious to our emotional make-up. We perpetually choose to fear God, for that has always been the standard of relationship with the "almighty."

The battle, the war within and without, consumes our sense of true self. The swords of religion are the daggers of words and concepts that enforce emotional fear and intellectual righteousness, trouncing upon the trembling birth of our spiritual enlightenment. What would it be like to feel a beneficent, peaceful god within our bodies? Could we conceive of it, and in light of what we know, would we choose it now?

We must search our mental faculties to find evolutionary perspectives of the many religious concepts that are holding us back. I have made a tentative list of some that we might alter or discard in view of our present realities and spiritual understanding. I do this as a way of seeking evolution, not as a point of argument destroying others' religious tenants or attacking one another's faith. Rather, I hope for a more harmonious level in which we can celebrate our collective awareness of a god, without the emphasis on our differences. What we "believe" about God is not as important as the embracing fact that we all care about and acknowledge a Divine Source, however we perceive it.

Here, then, are some concepts that are not conducive to our spiritual evolution. I wonder what others you might add?

The Concept of Original Sin

Creation mythology is as richly a part of collective consciousness as any other aspect of tribal heritage, and the creation tale of Adam and Eve is simply one of the early explanations for human existence. It is held sacred because all words chosen to be included in the Bible were "deemed" to be God's word, and therefore truth, rather than symbolic. Its truth is impossible within the scientific perspective of bodily understanding, and its symbolic imagery is anything but encouraging. The story of Adam and Eve as the source of all our travails is truly one of the most extraordinary twists of the human mind. Virtually every culture has a story about how humans came into being, and from the far corners of the earth we hear stories of how the first humans were imperfect or dissatisfied the gods that made them. There are always several attempts to create worthy humans before a level of adequacy is accomplished.

Typically, that imperfection has to do with human behavior and some form of punishment or exile that follows the inappropriate actions. Over and over again we see the carefully placed nuances that instill fear into the psyche, insuring submission to some overwhelming power. Whatever the story, it includes the negative whispers of our doom in the event of any independent action on our part.

I remember my grandfather telling the story of the bogeyman who came to eat little children that didn't behave and do what they were told. I could always tell that my "Pal" was trying to make sure we did what we were supposed to do. Independence is an unstable element in any institution and is carefully monitored by the "powers that be." Even at a very young age, I knew that this maneuver was about a power struggle, and my resistance only brought me a sense of being ostracized and not understood. I never believed him about the bogyman, but I often felt a bit sick to my stomach after he finished. I know he knew that I didn't believe him because I would make some rebellious remark, which seemed to very much annoy him.

Most children actually love those kind of spooky stories because feeling scared is kind of fun and adventuresome. Add them up throughout a childhood however, and you will have an adult addicted to the adrenaline rush, who cannot feel safe or peaceful in life and, in actuality, doesn't choose to. This kind of imprinting is an all-inclusive circle from parental training, through religious and societal programming. Controlling others by wielding the power of fear has always been the most effective weapon.

There is a glaring glitch in the Adam and Eve story that disturbs me. I am referring to the apple of knowledge of good and evil that Eve dared to pick, initiating "original sin." This predisposes the idea that evil already existed within the apple God had created and that the bad, seductive snake helped Eve to disobey God and fall from grace, knowing that it was there. Since God placed all the animals in the Garden, did he intend for the snake to tempt Eve? If so, then God set up an unsuspecting Eve with his own accomplice. For what purpose would he have done this? I cannot believe that God was tipping the scales to entice Eve to disobey so that she and Adam would be sent away.

Perhaps it really was about testing the human volition of free will. If so, God could have played out that particular chess game of potential without enlisting a human dupe such as Eve and igniting the fires of myth, whereby all women are waiting to lead men astray, and thus are not to be trusted or esteemed.

Did God really create evil beings such as the snake before Eve? Why would a god create evil? If this god somehow spawned de-evolutionary forces, then this god is not the ultimate Divine Source, but some imbalanced template polluted by galactic influences. Perhaps this is the root of our deepest imprints that humans and the world are not good, and therefore we must attempt to control our innate badness—or await our demise. Some people might say that evil is a great tool for growth.

I think this is old rhetoric and it is time to throw out these archaic, burdensome ways of learning. We do not have to find truth through suffering, nor do we need to be punished in order to learn how to be good. The laws of karma are always in play—the learning is the result of what occurs from the inside of our consciousness as we experience cause and effect—not from the outside. If we continue with the externalization of karmic laws, the rules and constrictions we perpetrate will ultimately neutralize and dissolve our free will—without which we cannot truly evolve. Evolution necessitates advancement of knowledge. What god would not wish its creation to learn and become imbued with wisdom?

The story of Adam and Eve links the apple with "carnal knowledge," meaning that somehow sexuality was a part of that evil. It is a poignant implication that humans were not to explore their bodies—the pleasure and procreation that were instilled in human biological and emotional DNA. Why would men and women have different bodies with genital organs if reproduction were not to take place in that way through them? How could it occur without some inherent pleasure to ensure the procreative act? It does—and that is a fact. In this unlikely scenario, I intuit a pollutive energy coming from the mind of man—not God.

Who wrote the book of Genesis? The old ones who compiled it certainly believed sexuality to be a dangerous and untamable force. Again, I sense a fear of sexual power emanating from a lower level of consciousness without any clarity or comprehension—not an edict from God who would not have created it in the first place if it were of no Divine use. What kind of trickery is this? Only one that could be dreamed up by unenlightened human consciousness. The Bible goes on to say that Adam and Eve then felt ashamed of their nakedness and God gave them fig leaves to cover themselves and their shame.

Isn't it fascinating to see that our pattern is to hide or cover our shame, our guilt—rather than overcome it or clear it? This reaction to their sexuality, and God's complicity to it, simply does not compute. Their shame would not have come from the apple of knowledge, but only from some conclusion that their bodies were displeasing to God. The story of Adam and Eve in the Bible is a conglomeration of emotionally charged edits that would not stand up to scrutiny if it were not for the fact that no one has ever questioned its authenticity from the beginning. Their guilt and shame are so innate to our own feelings that we easily believe in, and identify with them.

Adam and Eve are blamed for "original sin" because they supposedly disobeyed God. Through that act we are all condemned to hell without any merciful stay of execution unless we plead to be saved by our religion. While the law of karma demonstrates that the choices of our ancestors ripple down to us in ways that become our challenges to solve, they are not our "fault." To hold us to that could only be called manipulation. It seems much healthier to view Adam and Eve as a creation myth and not perpetuate the confinement of the human spirit in such a negative way.

The Concept of Obedience

This theme of obeying God, smacks of MAN. Here we see a projection onto The Divine that presumes a very personal and subjective relationship. Most religions today are still faltering under this belief that God is watching and marking the actions of humans so as to punish them for their misdeeds as if invested in their inherent weakness. Instilling us with the fear of non-obedience is a great way to control the believing hoards, but it is not worthy of, nor related to, the universal Divine Source. It was indubitably created by religions for the purpose of managing the masses.

If, indeed, free will were given to all creation, then there would not need to be such a personal, punitive reaction from God over human choices. In the end we **are** free, and every choice we make will teach us and thus further our evolution. We need not hold God to be the threatening deterrent for our misdeeds.

As an emerging species, we have not yet seen past the totem pole, vertical style of relationship in which there only exists who is above and who is below. Our parent/child repertoire has not opened the horizon of circular connection that allows each being to relate without the compliance factor of obedience to someone higher or more powerful. When will we master the art of cooperation and collective wisdom?

Islamic tradition embraces the law of surrender to Allah. If surrender could encompass the merging without resistance to The Divine within, it would be a truly magnificent principle. In its present stage, it refers to absolute compliance with the belief system of who and what Allah is. As Allah is seen through written interpretation, rather than direct knowing, surrender is diminished from a universal truth, to a cultural and encapsulated rendering of God.

Authority has always been a theme of the dominating masculine, while the feminine waits within the invisibility of potential, which will hopefully soon take its place. As we mature, inner knowing will release us from the grip of guesswork in terms of pleasing or obeying The Divine. Imagine a time when all our actions and choices will come from within us—no Homeland Security, no police force, no jails, no crime, because we will have activated an internal system of right and wrong that lies dormant within the fabric of our spiritual DNA.

The very concept of free will negates the prying, punishing God Force waiting to pronounce judgment upon the displeasing and disobeying masses. Only a god of limited power would need the obedience of its creation, and therefore concoct such a hell-ish shadow of Divine truth. One day we will see that our god is not only the lord of the heavens, but a more universal cosmic source. The Infinite needs nothing from us but the results of our embodiment as resource for the evolution of the Soul.

The Concept of Hell

This is one of the most negative imprints religions have wielded against humanity. It promotes the ancient perception of an angry God who created a terrible place of eternal pain and darkness to punish humans for wrongdoing. It seems possible, if not probable, that hell was introduced in ancient times as a weapon against non-compliance to religious authority in the same way that carnal brutality was used to frighten and control the masses. The idea that God will cast us away if we are not good is against all rational awareness. What we *do* in life is about how we learn the laws of karma—cause and effect, action and reaction, and therefore grow and evolve. Who we are is about the God Source and its creation.

We live in a reality of motion within the third dimension and forget the deeper aspects of cosmic truth that seem to elude our consciousness. We are Divine in essence and that cannot be changed. Punishment is not an advanced concept; it is a pathetic attempt to impede or control another being. Even if it is perceived as necessary for the good, it does not inspire or teach goodness, it breeds resentment and ill will. God has no need for it. Hell could not have been handed down from God; it was envisioned by man's own mind and through his vivid imagination, he has made it real!

Think of the command "burn in hell!" It carries the most violent condemnation with it. It offers no solace, no retraction, no possible treaty. The all-loving creative Source did not anchor hell into its evolving creation. People fear the fires of hell without any apparent consciousness of the source of their fear, because it is so ingrained in the psychogenetic fabric of our spiritual DNA. Un-accounted ancestors died with the condemnation of hell blasting through their cellular reality and we have inherited their fears intact.

We can create hell in many aspects of our daily existence simply because we see no way to free ourselves from the entrapment of our own darkest nightmares. Thus, we have transformed a concept of a place we come to after death into a state of being we live every day of our lives. We can change this morbidity by releasing hell from our genetic encoding (See Chapter12, *Technology of Consciousness*).

The Concept of Salvation
The idea that we need salvation from our inherent evil is as old as religion itself. It seems to be a deeply ingrained adjunct to the fear that we cannot please God, and therefore must be unworthy and "saved" from our own darkness. We have been

taught that God will grant us salvation from our original sin, but that salvation carries with it a host of rules about how to live in such a way as to be worthy of salvation in accordance with specific religious belief systems.

It is interesting that so many different religions hold this concept of salvation as the result of our sinful core, perpetrated by the ancestors and inherited psychogenetically by us. Though we may have some of their negative traits ingrained in us, we are not simple replicas of them. Their choices need not be ours and we need not become the victims of their deeds, or in other ways suffer for their lack of humanity.

God did not create us to then save us. The Divine Source created us to expand the potential of sacred life. Let us instead save ourselves from our own destruction, because we are capable of doing it and because we are evolving into a species that can not only rectify imbalances, but improve who we are on all levels. It is almost belittling of Jesus the Christ to label him "the savior." He did not seek to save us from evil; he spent his entire life on earth teaching the power of love and the grace of miracles. He asked us to do the same, and instead we have spent these two thousand years whimpering about being weak and unworthy, and pleading to be saved.

The salvation concept is flawed because it is an ultimatum, a threat of punishment in a future scenario if we do not find or ask for redemption. Salvation is tied to the concept of Judgment Day/heaven or hell. It presumes that without threat or force, we would not be good! While it is comforting to think that a religion can save us from ourselves and erase all wrongdoing so that in the end we will be safe, it does not help us to evolve spiritually; it just feeds our astute sense of expediency.

Wouldn't it be better to choose more enlightened ways of living now, rather than barter a future that we expect to be the doom of our existence? Where salvation interfaces with forgiveness and freedom from guilt, it becomes a joyful sense of new beginnings. Perhaps it is time to reverse this concept altogether. What if we were to contemplate "saving" God from the prison of our poisonous minds, our blindness to Divine possibility?

God the Father

God is seen in almost all religions as a father figure. When it comes to facing death or the universe, we can only imagine the strength to go on if we feel that a powerful energy we identify with fathering qualities could guide or protect us. The extension from an earthly parental father to a heavenly one brings a sense of safety and comfort.

We are raised with the need to please and obey our earthly father so the concept of doing the same for our "heavenly father" is part of how we expect to relate to him and why we so readily accept the edicts of our churches. Our ancient concept of the angry, vengeful god is also played out within this portrayal of god the father that causes us to be fearful. This anxiety about pleasing him enhances the role of male religious leaders as intermediaries between humans and their Divine Source.

We still want someone to "lord" it over us, tell us what to do, save us from our weaknesses, and in short, take responsibility for our lives. We have always asked and expected males to do this, but we have never allowed their truly spiritual, gentle energies to also be experienced as strong. If over the millenniums those deeper qualities had developed, perhaps religious wrath would not have taken the fore. Because we now have reached an octave wherein we can not only destroy human lives but also our own home planet, we must face the realization that we are here to use free will as part and parcel of our destiny, and must now rebalance our spiritual expression in such a way as to catalyze the evolution of our Souls. It is not such a terrible thing to free God from the role of father and instead take up the staff of authority ourselves.

Monotheism

The dominant religious concept today is that of monotheism; although, numerous cultures such as the Egyptians, Mayans, Hindus, Greeks, pagans and others related to many gods. I see that fracturing as the individuation of Divine presence into themes of survival that were personalized by a form representing specific aspects and needs. It is much like the way doctors and other professionals today specialize in their fields. A god of rain, of fertility, prosperity, etc., crystallized the facets of their necessities without the focus on an integrated wholeness. The most difficult aspect of this idea is that each god required appeasement, sacrifice and some form of adulation.

If all these "lesser" gods were under a larger one god, it might help us to close the gap of separation. Unfortunately, the element of jealousy and ownership introduced in the Old Testament caused us to perceive that all gods would be jealous of each other just as we ourselves experience that kind of envy today. Therefore, we have invested in a one and only god. If we thought of the one god not as the *only* Divine energy, but rather that all beings of heavenly stature are expressions of that oneness, then it would be easier to feel our relationship to all beings as spiritual in nature—including humans. It is what the Hindus call Brahman.

Our battles over whose god is the only one have created so much bloodshed and death that they have overshadowed the true meaning of The Divine. We must begin to recognize that at least some of our fervor is more about our supremacy over others than it is about God. We see God as an extension of ourselves and only within our own cultural reality, rather than ourselves as a Divine expression that goes beyond our own repertoire.

It is possible that the one god we worship is only the highest representation that we can conceive of now—there may be infinitely higher forms of that oneness! What illumination will our children bring us from the far reaches of the universe? It is infinitely more magnificent to imagine a god that encompasses it all than a limited god whose sole domain is our present world. As we evolve, so will our relationship with the Divine Source—all that is needed is our choice to expand our consciousness.

In the end, it is not whether there is only one god that seems relevant to me, but rather how we relate to The Divine. The passionate sense of loyalty that monotheism beseeches, too often excludes the infinite faces and forms of The Divine. If we could relate to everyone as part of that essence, God would be a focal point of peace and spiritual oneness.

God and Abundance
Money and faith are a formidable force. The power of money to sway reality has been in play since the genesis of religion,

and the subsequent wealth of churches has allowed them to bend and shape whole kingdoms. God as a business is a lucrative endeavor; one that has been wielded with great success in virtually every society on the planet.

The intertwining of money and religion occurs everywhere, and even though Western societies are criticized for their blatant materiality, all religions engage in the "buying and selling" of spirit. In India, the jewel of eastern spirituality and non-material perspective, I remember how each ritualistic gesture necessitated some recompense. Whether it was a red dot on the forehead or entrance to a temple, there was a required exchange—from the rich and the poor alike. Why not? Should we not offer something to those who hold the space for our religious endeavors to be supported? Absolutely!

Many churches require the law of tithing or pledging a certain amount of money to the church, a concept of division or compartmentalizing life by clear boundaries—so much for the self, so much for the church. The incongruence lies more in our pretense that spirituality has nothing to do with abundance and disfavors it, while we use that very same energy to influence our relationship with God through our offerings to the church.

There is a fine line between the investing and supporting of one's church and buying favors to appease God, assuage guilt, annul marriages, receive indulgences, erase sin, get into heaven and other negotiations through the mediation of church officials that are blatant manipulations of religious guidelines. When did this begin? It was insidious from the very first breath of organized religion. When will it end? The time is now for us to see clearly what is true about money and how it relates to the un-manifest universe, as well as our world in which it has historically influenced the power of religious authority, not only over its constituents, but also by influencing all manor of governing bodies.

The interweaving of church and state can be very insidious. In Germany, Christians must pay the government special religious taxes, which the government then funnels off to the churches. Consider the expense of such a convoluted arrangement; the waste of money in administration that benefits no one. It is rumored that soon it may be legally impossible to "quit" a church to avoid these taxes. The concept of levying taxes on people in the name of their religion seems archaic, but in fact, has been in practice since the earliest of times.

However, as we acknowledge that there is "the business of God," we must see to it that it does not continue to be something hypocritical or abused by those who promote the virtues of poverty while raking in the spoils of guilt. The problem comes in that churches preach poverty as a way to God while becoming rich in the preaching. The idea that God loves a poor person as a compensation for not having the basics of what one needs is a pretense for covering the inequalities that all institutionalized churches need to address.

The concept of poverty as a path to holiness began in the Western world with St. Francis of Assisi and the edict of the Pope's Bull of 1206 in which he spoke of imitating Christ's poverty and "to go humbly in search of heretics and lead them out of error." Of course, in so doing, great wealth was stripped from people and handed over to the church while offending rivals were conveniently eliminated through inquisitions, et cetera. St. Francis' joy was to forsake the external world of materialism in which he found his merchant father, and others caught—to a life of giving and sharing. It was a very cathartic experience for him to amend the pain of slaughter after coming home from the Crusades by enacting his true, gentle nature.

These sentiments to live as did Christ are inspirational even today, but they have bred a false equation in which money is bad and wealth suspect of conniving trickery. There is no room for the potential goodness that abundance could bring if used as a gift for all. When we learn this lesson of sharing, we will "break bread" and humans will be ready to move to a new octave of manifesting abundance.

According to the Old Testament, the lord literally demanded "ransom" for man's Soul in exchange for protection. "When thou takest the sum of the children of Israel after their number, then shall they give everyman a ransom for his soul unto the LORD, when thou numberest them; that there be no plague among them" (Exodus 30:11-12). That the ransom was one of material substance seems completely incongruent with the spirit of Divine exchange and the seduction of protection, irresistible. When a plague or other travesty hit them, I am sure the religious leaders found a way to make the people believe that God was punishing them for their sinful ways rather than that the Lord did not keep his end of the bargain.

What a poisonous concept—that man must pay for the redemption of his Soul! A Divine Soul cannot be spoiled even though a body may engage in every manor of misdeeds. This lord of old was instilling the "buying and selling" imprint at the very core of religion! In effect, this is a message that implies our Souls are something that we can barter! Worse yet, is that we barter them with God who could somehow take them away from us. Today we use the language, "He sold his Soul," meaning that he will do anything to get what he wants or thinks he needs. No! Humans were given a Divine spark—Soul of the One Soul, and it cannot be revoked by anyone—not even the creator. Intrinsic in that design was free will, the power of knowledge through choice!

I loved the story in the Bible of Jesus going into the temple and driving out the moneylenders, the corrupt and insidious forces that had taken over the sacred place of devotion. That is what time it is now! We must revise the relationship between God and our finances, our political systems and our perception of truth wherein money has become the source of miracles, the chamber of torture, the illusion of heaven on earth. Jesus did not live poor as a statement of virtue to the multitudes, he had a mission to quicken the human DNA and advance our species by bringing teachings about the power of love—to everyone. He did not condemn wealth, he taught the principles of sharing. He broke the bread, multiplied the fish, changed the water into wine to demonstrate that we also could do these things so that our consciousness could be free to expand and explore the unseen worlds and the cosmic laws of energy—without opposing the needs of the body.

Buddha brought the knowledge of nirvana, the state of enlightenment beyond attachment to worldly things. He renounced his birthright of wealth because he saw that nothing material could heal human suffering, and so he went in search for a higher truth. Both Buddha and Christ came to take us beyond the limitation of physical law. Neither had need of material wealth, because they both carried the infinite radiance of the universe and taught about its potential as a part of our world. To think that we cannot be wealthy both physically and spiritually is a judgment of limitation upon us all, sourced within our own mental and emotional fragilities. Though we are indeed seduced by the flashy material world, the whispers of our Souls are ever guiding us home to our spiritual source— the richest possession of all!

The concept that money is not spiritual has become a point of great confusion in every culture. For some, money could be a karma that invites them to rebalance themes about compassion or sharing; for others money may be the teaching about power or receiving. In effect, there is no theme in our lives that does not touch upon our karmic, spiritual evolution. It is never the "thing" itself, but rather how we wield all potential that is presented to us. Unimagined changes are coming!

That money or wealth will take us away from God or distract us so that we forget the Divine Source, stems from the illusion that we can only pay attention to one thing at a time. This is no longer true. Though it has seemed true in the past, it was due to the fact that humans were swallowed in greed and not truly connected to the kind of expansive cosmos that touches our consciousness now. We are learning to "multitask" and that relates to all levels of our consciousness.

We are now beginning to stretch our minds out far enough to follow the circular path of the law of manifestation. "What goes out comes back" has been told us for millenniums, but we have not understood it deeply enough to practice it, certainly not without some hope of reimbursement or acknowledgement. Most importantly, until now we had not discovered the power of giving. When we extend our wealth to support others, we exercise our potential to change reality for the better.

In truth, few of us actually hold ourselves in enough regard to imagine that we could be the givers—that we could let go of what we have enough to share it without thinking we would be taken advantage of, or somehow lose our place in the pecking order of power. Fortunately, a new breed of givers is opening our awareness to this power today. Look at Bill and Melinda Gates, who are using their wealth to balance and improve the quality of life for people everywhere. It seems that the more they give, the more comes to them. This has always been a part of the law of abundance; the more you give, the more you receive—on many levels. We need only to come to the realization that abundance is a form of grace to be shared and utilized for all, and that there is abounding joy connected to the giving.

All Life is Suffering
This is the pronouncement of the Buddha who sought to deliver humans from the sorrows of painful existence on physical and emotional levels. He taught that we could reach to a heightened state of non-attachment called nirvana. While the awareness that this world is not the only or even truest reality may encourage us to let go of our attachments, it does not help us embrace life's experiences in such a way as to alter evolution. We are here and it is not a punishment, it is an opportunity. Though we may be on a perpetual cycle of reincarnation, the concept that returning to the wheel of karma is negative does not include Divine purpose. We do not return

only to rebalance our faulty existence, we return to amplify the evolution of ourselves, and the Divine Source.

All life is **not** suffering. Although it may not be the cosmic inertia of non-embodiment, it is the opportunity of evolution through living and experiencing that expands all possibilities—throughout the universes. It is our choice to become fully enlightened, sentient beings by living in body and through those experiences, furthering the infinite pool of psychogenetic encoding. As we awaken to an expanded consciousness that includes all inheritance through ancestors, as well as multi-incarnations, we will clearly see the magnificent possibilities before us. We suffer because we do not know!

As we become aware, we will see that suffering is not the handmaiden of life, it is the illusion that we have no free will, and therefore cannot choose to embrace all experience from a point of grace and the power of the giver. We have come—not only to rebalance misdeeds, but because we have something to offer life from our most pure and Divine Soul!

Religious concepts have been handed down through generations of religious leaders without the possibility of alteration, because the intrinsic nature of connecting to the God Source *conceptually* has always been the prevailing path. There is a terrible blockage in this system that forces a crystallized structure of God into religious foundation, and then cannot find a way through that density to a more loving and applicable spiritual experience, which is so desperately needed. If we can move into a more elevated experiential format and truly have the courage to look at those concepts that support us today—and those that do not—we will be able to bring religion with us into a new era of expanded reality.

EVOLUTION

1. Review and contemplate your own religious concepts and look deeply into how they have affected your life. (See Chapter 11, *Tracking Your Own Spiritual Repertoire.*)

2. Choose to hold in your heart that all humans are Divine and good in their essence, not sinners or Divine rejects.

3. Release the fear of hell. (See Chapter 12, *Technology of Consciousness.*)

4. Meditate on the presence and energy of the Divine Source—beyond human form.

5. Open yourself to all the wealth of the universe and trust that you have the power to be the giver.

6. Release the addiction to suffering and become conscious of your gift to life and this world.

SIX

MOLDING THE MASSES

IN THE SAME WAY THAT PARENTS MOLD their children by threatening punishment for misbehavior, religions mold their followers by laying down the rules to live by and then threatening consequences if those rules are not followed. Being labeled "bad" is hurtful to us all at any age. Children are certainly impressed by the possibility of corporal punishment or restriction of freedom, but perhaps no less so by the possibility of being struck down by God or the fear of damnation and hell. Most children are given this punishment/retribution tale from an early age. The mind is so vivid and fertile that the thought of the devil, the fires of hell, Judgment Day, or reckoning for our sins is enough to temper our actions.

Yet, we have become somewhat numb in our everyday awareness of this conditioning and have developed the habit of going through the motions of repentance, assigning ourselves a degree of guilt and then continuing on with whatever it is that we are doing. We go to church but we aren't really present because we have learned to shut out threatening condemnations. Nevertheless, our fear of retribution from God moves like a plague in our inner core and is passed on psychogenetically to our children, as if it were a parasite leaching off our spiritual DNA.

The word repent carries such a heavy connotation that it is even repulsive to most of us. It is not that we shouldn't be sorry, or are not sorry for any misdeeds; it is that repentance is tied to such an overall heaviness of unspecified guilt that we feel crushed by its weight. Lurking behind the word is the threat of all the tortuous results religion can hurl at us if we do not repent. It is essential for us to take responsibility for our actions from our deepest knowing, from our awareness of what is right and true, but not by coercion.

Repentance is a cry that echoes from the pulpits of most denominations around the world. Imagine the power of such energy being blasted out to hundreds, thousands, and even millions of people via television. The masses who attend revivals and huge church gatherings are not only bombarded with the accusing words of the officiates, but by the negative energy spewing from the crowds as they release thoughts and feelings of guilt and shame. They may feel relieved by their repentance, but the energy of its source has seeped even deeper into their psychogenetic makeup.

It is much easier to shout about the need to repent than it is to speak gently about our goodness. I remember how I loved beating my chest in Catholic mass and repeating in Latin, "mea culpa, mea culpa." It seemed clean and powerful. But when I contemplated its meaning in English, "my fault, my fault," it had a different ring. It seemed to carry with it the implication that *everything* was my fault. I could take responsibility for my own actions, but I could not feel that the "sins" of the world—past or present—were mine. It is not about innocence or blame; it is about a sense of balance and truth.

The echoes of sin and judgment that have become entrenched in our minds and hearts bind us to a false understanding of our creator. Judgment Day is wielded by Jews, Christians and Muslims alike as the impetus to be good in life in order to avoid the punishment that will most certainly be meted out by God on that terrifying day of reckoning. I once had a vivid experience of that possibility when I was in the Peace Corps at the age of twenty-two. I was told that it was almost certain I would die before morning when the surgeon could get to the field hospital where I lay. Taking in that probable reality, I began having spontaneous flash backs of every negative or guilty thought, word and deed I had committed beginning from the time I was less than two years old! Each of these vignettes was stored in the mind of the cells and I recalled them from the perspective of my body at the moment each occurred. I would not have needed any external force to condemn me, because I had already done so and I was astounded at the amount of self-judgment I held in my body.

I have pondered for a long time how I became contaminated with the threat of judgment and damnation. My early memories of Sunday school where of pretty pastel pictures of lambs and lights in the clouds and sayings we memorized, such as "God is love." However, I remember that as I grew older and went to various churches—Christian and non-Christian, I heard repeatedly the warnings about the terrible things in store for "us sinners." I sensed that this was the usual adult ploy of control and manipulation and it still surprises me that even though my conscious mind recognized the fallacies, it had no apparent power to override the subtle subconscious imprints.

I have no doubt that our fearful, guilty minds have collectively created the wrenching shadows of purgatory and the eternal darkness of hell; but I have always known instinctively that it existed only by our own design—not God's. In fact, I have had an actual experience of purgatory that has helped me to see how the mind creates reality. I have seen the hellish dark energies exuding up from those who exist in the shadow zones of purgatory and hell, and have also heard accounts by hundreds of others telling their own stories.

In this lifetime, I have had six near-death experiences, and in one of them I experienced what the Catholics call purgatory. It was a car accident. As my body lay crumpled on the ground, my spirit drifted downward into a very dark place. A profound and frightening blackness swept over me and then I heard odd and seemingly angry sounds coming closer and closer. A multitude of shadowy figures pushed at me with a forceful energy and spoke in mass,

"You can't come here!"
"You can't come here!"

Incredulously, I recognized a person I had known who died in a car accident the year before. I am sure that the karmic tie with her, which provided the magnetic link into that dark space, was the fear of car accidents that had come from her death. I had the horrifying sense that all of them felt they would dwell there forever, and therefore claimed it as their territory. From the density of their energy, I know that no god put them there, but that they sent themselves into this state of purgatory because it was actually what they expected to happen to them.

The woman I had known stepped forward and shoved me backward with her arm. I cannot describe that push. It wasn't something of touch, but it had an energetic strength and unhooking effect that I will never forget.

I remember the sensation of moving upward and suddenly I found myself inside a kind of rainbow bubble surrounded by infinite translucent others. A sensation of what I would call all-encompassing love flowed into and around me, and I felt connected to a kind of vastness that had no end. Some might say, "embraced in the arms of God," but there was no sense of personal individualization, just pure consciousness. There was an awareness of an energetic transmission in which I was shown the secrets of life, the interconnectedness of the form-less and the form. It was the "relativity" that Einstein talked about in which everything is related or connected, and that connection has a synergistic purpose.

In my work I have come across many trapped spirits who died in sudden shock and became entwined in lower astral realms we would call purgatory. They have forgotten the light and mechanically repeat the suffering of their deaths and the self-punishment they were taught would befall them for their "sins."

Religion has hoisted upon us that we are sinners "against God" because of what we do, and that we will be punished for it. Yes, we may act or live out of harmony with Divine law, be blinded by pain or religious perspective, but our trans-gressions are against ourselves; they are not directed toward God. Our damnation and darkness are our own and we suffer greatly from them.

The ceremonies, rituals and special events of religions cast a binding spell upon their participants, and to various degrees— mold their lives. While it is glorious that everyday life could be interrupted by celebration of sacred passages, the deeper meaning of many such actions are, in fact, contrary to spiritual truth. Baptism, for example, would be wonderful as a ceremony in which the parents and family are brought into the pure and holy state of a newborn, just arrived from the unmanifest realms of The Divine. They should be blessed and purified to receive such a miraculous gift as a child who is absolutely within the state of grace. The pure Soul in the body of the child need not be saved, but for the old saw of human sin. It is unfathomable to me that we were created in imperfection. (What a slander of the creative force!) Such a concept must definitely be a throwback to the mythologies of ancient, unenlightened minds.

Baptism seems to be a joyous welcoming to our world, but the insidious undertone of its blessing is saving the un-baptized child from the religiously perpetrated threat of the jaws of hell. The actual purpose of baptism is to wash away "original sin." Dogma relates that all humans are born with original sin and that only those who are baptized can escape its taint. That mandate would certainly inspire all parents to make sure their child is baptized.

The church has conveniently put forth that anyone not baptized will suffer the fires of hell, and thus many people who have not been baptized choose to do so when they are in mortal peril from illness or age, because fear of Divine retribution is so deeply ingrained in them. If we could now release the illusion of original sin, we could pass from our bodies knowing that only Divine energy will touch us.

The ceremonies of confirmation, Bar Mitzvah and others, are given as indoctrination to specific belief systems. They bring with them the cloak of religious belonging, even if the young person did not actually ask for it themselves. They believe because we want them to believe, and they want to be loved and accepted by us. In these moments of religious passage, we reign supreme in our families, receiving gifts and honor and being truly accepted. It is no wonder that there is such a deep sense of guilt and separation when later in life we want to go on from those innocent realities and shed some of those beliefs that we no longer hold true. It is as if we can never return to those precious moments, as if we were traitors on some level to our families and ourselves.

Even patterns of speech keep the faithful in their rightful place of submission to religious authority. Listen to the subtle message given from a priest when he addresses his parishioner as "my child." It seems to be a protective endearment that engenders a sense of pleasing God and church. People are comforted when spoken to in that way, but it is also a patronizing and diminishing way of perpetrating the totem pole structure of religious might—though in all probability, the priest is oblivious to its derogation. He actually considers his "flock" as children—uninitiated in the mysteries of God because they have not studied religious doctrine. The most profound, naturally spiritual Souls simply are not registered on his perceptual screen.

Likewise, the term "children of God" is a reference to our unenlightened status. At some point we must release these superficial connotations of who we are. This child identity stems from the same ancient framework in which humans could only see God through their familial repertoire of father to children—"He sent his only begotten son." The world was small then and lives pivoted around tight family groupings. There were few points of reference for relationships and they were bound in vertical patterns of power.

Yes, we are a young species, but we bring with us the wisdom of evolution, of Divine consciousness and the mandate to take responsibility for our realities and our world. We are mired in our habit of excuses and blame. We cannot forever pretend that what is happening in our homes, our environment, our world, is not us—it is! It is time we let go of being the children in all levels of our lives—we have the power. Were we not given the mandate to create heaven on earth?

From the earliest of times, new religious systems borrowed marks of identity from the old so as to make it easier to implant their beliefs, and the signposts of different religions are the sights and sounds that express them. We are conditioned to react to the sight of the cross, the smell of incense, the forms and shapes we have assigned religious meaning. The flicker of candles, the sound of prayers, chants and songs all help us to connect with our religions, and are extremely effective as tools for molding the masses into the adherents churches need for their own survival. The statues, paintings, altars, crosses, and even the architecture become the hallmarks of how we identify ourselves spiritually.

All religious institutions use paraphernalia to augment the power of their dogma and religious authority. Religious paraphernalia such as ankhs, rosaries, malas, bands, etc., all help us remember to pray and to think of God. We like the trappings, but it is important to review their meaning—to listen to the words of our prayers and see if they are aligned with our hearts' knowing.

We have always created interpretive mental structures as a way to segue between the tangible and intangible realities around us. They are the language we use as humans to comprehend what our minds conceive.

How can we teach ourselves to feel the Divine Source inside us without the bombardment of external props? It is as if we are so programmed to artificial stimuli that we might not include The Divine in our lives without it. Yet, the sacredness of life exudes from all of nature and mirrors our own intrinsic spirituality. As we evolve, we will be able to feel that divinity as part of our being, we will not need to represent it in form; or most probably, form itself will metamorphose into a more holographic, multidimensional presence that we will cognate from new levels of perception.

Perhaps the most powerful form of molding the masses is through the mental concepts we are given. Heaven and hell are very vivid in our imaginations and certainly move in and out of our outer consciousness throughout our lives. All religions speak of a place of afterlife that is far better than the place we inhabit now and if we only follow the dictates of our religion we might reach that place. We have rich images of angels and harps, celestial clouds, heaven and beautiful scenes given us by religious artists that amplify our connection and desire to make afterlife our ultimate goal.

Once we become aware that we have been molded, we can see its effects in the subtle choices we make and the conclusions that follow. Consciousness of this molding process can untangle us from negative imprints and help us to free ourselves from the clutch of control.

If religious doctrine has forged an indelible imprint of human frailty or evil, then we must find a way to break out of its mold or we will never discover the magnificent goodness we hold inside us. I think fondly of my tiny granddaughter offering me her food—so simple, so truly human. Why cannot we do this as adults? We shun the sight of hunger in the world and pretend it is not about us—it is! These are the initiations of humans to test our worthiness, not how many prayers, not the self-righteousness of counting what we are owed in return for favors, not our attendance at church, not who we have convinced to join our religion.

EVOLUTION

1. Meditate on any ways you have been molded religiously that are no longer true for you—then release them. (See Chapter 12, *Technology of Consciousness.*)

2. Search out and release any religious imprints that cause you to adhere to dogma out of fear. (See Chapter 12, *Technology of Consciousness.*)

3. Trace your memory back to the first time in this lifetime that you remember being told about purgatory or hell. Release any imprints.

4. Release any energies related to repentance that make you feel unworthy.

SEVEN

Churches Today

B UOYED BY OUR STAGNANT RELIGIOUS CONCEPTS, our church experiences today have become confined mostly to habitual, prefabricated formats that ingrain guilt and fear, rather than inspiration. Sermons are filled with negative rhetoric that lowers heads and squeezes hearts. We hear about the deeds of saints but cannot find a way to truly connect to them, perhaps because sainthood has always been intertwined with great suffering. The threat of Armageddon and the end of it all has become a church formula for healing our sins, but invariably numbs our consciousness to the possibilities of true enlightenment. Hell and Judgment Day are not remedies to be taken in large quantities. They have, in fact, become a slow poisoning of the human race.

We have come to believe deeply within our subconscious minds that damnation is what we deserve, because we are not "good enough" for our parents, our god—or ourselves. This shadow of self-doubt has been cast by religion and the negative imprinting that has darkened our hearts must be lifted by a new spiritual order that supports our Divinity, not our damnation!

A diet of unconditional love and consciousness is what we need now; it is the feast set before us by the great templates of Divine truth. All the founders of religions have held qualities of compassion, mercy and wisdom that modeled life beyond the level of struggle, to a template of grace. Their lives inspired us even down through the ages, but their spiritual paths have been muddied by the trodden feet of those who could not walk in their stead, could not emulate their teachings, and therefore brought them through the filter of their own repertoire. It is now our turn to interpret the true message of the Divine Source and how it interplays within our daily lives. We must do this for ourselves.

If churches were willing to revamp their religious concepts and the way they are presented to the faithful in a more timely and uplifting manner, perhaps the experience of going to church could become a new, more enlightening adventure. I am not saying that we must throw out our belief system or stop attending religious services, I am saying that religious leaders must help us break free of the limited assumptions of our ancestors and worship/relate to God from a present day consciousness.

I wonder if it were not for the threats of hell and fear of judgment, how many people would actually go to church today, except on religious holidays. We need our holidays for many reasons beyond their original religious context. Millions of people only enter their churches because of social and familial pressure impinging upon them, especially during holiday seasons. Almost everyone has an emotional tie to spiritual holidays because of the associative memories of touching God, feeling part of a family, of gifts, and especially the wonderful food that is shared during those gatherings. These memories are binding on the sense of self and we rarely outgrow them unless they are replaced with something similar yet more truthful.

So many people go to their place of worship on Christmas, Easter, Passover, and spend their entire time feeling guilty that they have not been there since the last holiday. They promise themselves they will come "back to the fold"—knowing deep within that they cannot. Why? Most often it is about the guilt they feel, because they really do not believe in the sermons or enjoy the hanging of the head, the secrets of the hypocrite, or the sense of unworthiness attached to a long list of transgressions—typically brought up to them in the sermon.

Too many of our holidays are about atonement of sins, observance of our failings or the wrongs done to God by our forefathers. The Jews atone for the wickedness of Abraham's children; a cultural mandate in which "the sins of the fathers are visited upon the children." The atonement came from an era in which generations were close together because of short lives and the limitations of travel. It is time for us to stop atoning for the deeds of our ancestors. The only thing to lament here is that we may have inherited such negative imprints of humans.

Despite the inhuman things we are still perpetrating against each other, we are goodness in our core and we are learning. Anne Frank, the famous young Jewish girl, wrote in her diary before she was sent to the gas chambers by the Nazis, "I still believe that humans are really good at heart." Jesus the Christ brought the consciousness of love two thousand years ago and it has taken these millennia to begin the process of exploring love's potential, or living it. Anne Frank, a girl of fifteen, understood it all. Let us not discover it in the same devastating fashion as did she!

So many people ask me what they should do about the "this way or that way" dilemma they feel in terms of leaving their churches or trying to make "faith" the glue that holds them to their religions. They feel faith in God but not in their churches, and the demand to take everything that no longer seems true to them—on faith. I always suggest that they find the highest teachings that support their lives and practice them—without guilt about religious dogma or church attendance. The most powerful and true answers come from our own heart, our inner voice—the Higher Self. Above all, we must learn to hear that voice and trust ourselves as to whether we want to continue going to church, believing in our religions, or not.

As we evolve our concepts of God, we will be able to make worship more beautiful, more meaningful. The wealth of our religious endeavors has been poured into the construction of magnificent churches that inspire us with the awe of God's omnipotence. The places of worship created by every religion are of spectacular beauty either through their opulence, structural design, or by the sacredness of their natural setting. It is in concert with our highest energies to create such magnificent places in which we can feel that we are entering "the house of God," lavishing our riches, our hopes and our prayers on this house so we will feel we are honoring God, and in our hope that the Divine Source will come to us, help us.

Imagine a cathedral, mosque or temple hundreds of years old in which thousands of people have come to pray, to beseech God, to be comforted for their sorrows or sins. The wailing echoes of human suffering psychically permeate the floors, walls and ceilings to such a degree that they are palpable to anyone who is sensitive to emotions. It could be that we feel their sadness as a heavy curtain of debt to God. That heaviness is often perceived as true spiritual energy, and so we whisper and hold our breath in grave respect for this holy place. Why do we think that seriousness is more sacred than joy or celebration? Most people who enter such places sense the solemnity of religious enactment but do not realize that part of its energy belongs to those who have released their guilt and emotional baggage into the depository of their church, and thus created its heavy atmosphere.

We can use our **consciousness** to lift the weight of this curtain so we can experience sacredness beyond the emotions of sorrow or the past. Imagine being able to wipe away the tears and suffering that have energetically covered our places of worship! Let me show you how to do this with the technology of consciousness—right here and now. First, read through this exercise so that you know what to do.

You will do this with your eyes closed.

Allow yourself to project your awareness into a church through your mind's eye. Perhaps it is the place you go every week or one you visited, or ask your Higher Self (your own intuitive, inner voice) to focus your awareness on one for you—it could even be a church structure of another religion!

Focus on the negative energies that need to be washed away or erased. You may become aware of their specific qualities such as guilt, fear, shame, sorrow, et cetera. You might feel them emanating from the corners, ceiling, floors or even the pews or alter.

Imagine a brilliant white beam of light coming through the top of your head and radiating out from your stomach/solar plexus and back out into the sky. This clears your own energy field so that you do not pick up any negative energy as you are engaged in this exercise.

Now ask the energies that have become encrusted in the church what color (frequency of light) they need to be transmuted and released?

Take the first color or colors that come into your consciousness and imagine that you are drawing them from the cosmos, down through the top of your head, down through your heart, and into your stomach/solar plexus.

From there, laser them out into the places that are holding the old energies. You may need to beam the colored frequency throughout the entire area. Feel the light passing effortlessly through you and out, until you sense a shifting of the energy. It will seem lighter in the whole area to which you have been sending color. You will sense a change in your own energy; an uplifting quality that brings a kind of peace to you.

You are finished. Take a deep breath and open your eyes. It is that simple. You have just given an immense gift to all those who enter there and even to those whose spirits are entrapped, as well! Thank you.

Two main activities are pivotal in places of worship—sermons and prayer. Sermons can be the catalysts of change or the lethal dosages of rhetoric. Sometimes when I listen to political speeches I am amused by how similar they are to sermons. I am almost certain that politicians unwittingly copy their authoritative preaching style from their religious leaders. They both seem to hook the audience by exploitation of possible dire outcomes of the present path and invariably include villains and promises. Even the raising of the fist, the pointing of the finger, the puffing up of the chest, and the righteous glare of the eye seem to be copies of each other. The rise and fall of the voice produces a studied format of emphasis that carries the audience onto a wave of hypnotic trance that is only broken when the sermon or speech ends.

From the time I was a child, I "saw" that after about three minutes of sermon, a great number of the people would click off their attention and mentally wander in an absent minded way while looking at the walls, ceilings, or statues. It was as if they could not really listen to the sermon any further. Sometimes they would even stare at the pulpit with a fixed gaze, pretending to pay rapt attention, but I could "hear" them thinking about their problems, what they wanted to do as soon as church was over, and even about dinner.

This lapse of concentration stems from the content of sermons preached in pulpits. So much of what is said is simply not what we experience to be true in our lives or embarrassingly not what we live. They are all too often reminiscent of parental preaching that we would like to forget. The threats of old do not have as much power over us as they once did—perhaps we are so busy in the outer world that even hell will have to wait! It is not gone from our psyche, but rather lurks there beneath our conscious awareness causing confusion and self-doubt. These negative energies are very destructive, because they hold us within the patterns of survival causing the vicious circle of desperation, survival action, justification and guilt.

Preaching is sometimes hard to listen to even if we agree with the essence of what is being said, but suffer from the negativity of its energetic message or flinch at the interpretation being presented by the preacher. There may come a day in the future when preaching will simply not occur in the formal sense, and may be replaced with a new design of loving communion that brings us all together into the energy of the Divine Source.

Through it all, we have begun to think on our own, and life is hard enough without a constant reminder that we will surely go to hell anyway. We are no longer naughty children who must be scolded and punished for not being "good enough." Worship should make us feel good about ourselves! We should be able to feel our direct connection to the Divine Source and be supported as we come together to experience all that is sacred and to celebrate that we are part of it. We need to feel encompassed and embraced by unconditional love that would bring us back to church again and again without badgering or cajoling or the condemning tactics from anyone outside us, including the religious leaders to whom we have supposedly given permission to guard our Souls!

In truth, watching people respond to sermons was the most fascinating part of churchgoing for me from the time I was very small. I wanted to see what they felt so I could see if I were right in perceiving that all the talk was just a way to make us do what the preacher wanted. I was curious as to why people bowed their heads in church. I knew that it was about respect because everyone did it in all the churches, but I felt that it was partly about being ashamed and unworthy. It occurs to me that if we collectively changed the bowing of the head to lift the face and heart upwards, we would more easily access the bliss that can come from communion with the Divine Source.

I was exposed to many kinds of churches and various religions, but the awe-inspiring sense of The Divine rarely occurred within church walls. Rather, it was in nature where it seemed I could stretch my consciousness freely and feel the mysterious presence of "God" everywhere and in everything. It wasn't the active kind of outdoors stuff of hiking, climbing, or canoeing to get somewhere far enough away from the world to have a spiritual experience; it was more the Ferdinand the Bull kind of sitting and smelling the flowers with that quiet smile on the face—what the world today would call meditation—or even Samadhi. I would pass through a state of heightened consciousness where I was aware of sights and sounds happening a long way away. Sometimes I would find myself out of body, moving and experiencing without any third dimensional constraints, sometimes into a nothingness or void, sometimes into an awareness that included all of my seventy senses of perception.

I do remember loving to be invited to High Mass at Catholic churches where the incense, candles and singing would draw me out of my body up into the golden, arched ceilings where I felt a kind of joyous freedom. I loved the back and forth in Latin between the priest and participants. Perhaps what made it so wonderful was that it was nothing like daily reality; nothing that had to do with social decorum or any conversation with those around me—it was simply free flight into the center of my being where I felt at home and filled with love.

You have done this too, you may have just forgotten. These memories carry such a high rate of vibration that we do not hold them in our awareness. It is the kind of work we do at The Light Institute. Over the last twenty-odd years, I have witnessed thousands of people enter into these memory capsules and that is how I know that **everyone** has these experiences. They were buried because they did not fit into the religious format we were taught—i.e., you go to church to find God—it isn't really an authorized, independent option to touch God in any other format.

There are many priests and preachers today from all over the world who are attempting to inspire their constituents with more positive interpretations of religious concerns, but the underlying belief systems are the same, and therefore cannot really offer a way through the boundaries of dogma.

The second main ingredient of religious service is prayer. There is something very beautiful about praying in groups. Whether we are praying in song, words, or silently, communal prayer creates a special, sacred energy that brings us up onto a higher octave of consciousness. The communion that is created when we pray together allows us to release the smallness of our individual selves and amplifies the power of oneness that is a deep, essential part of our human nature. The quality of collective prayers is more inspiring because the themes are usually about peace, healing, and the love of God, rather than individual needs.

There have been many studies proving that prayer is in fact beneficial to healing. Is it that God answers our prayers, or is it that the power of our focused consciousness taps into our Divine Source and brings forth the same healing energy that is innate in all of life because it was seeded into creation by

Source? I think it is the latter and that we can not only call to us these healing energies from the God Source, but as we do, we can actually transmit this energy to someone while activating it in them, as well. We are sending them Divine healing energy and their own healing capacities are also kicked on. It is a double dose of healing that will help them to reset the energies in their bodies, but above all, it is a choice of their Soul to heal or not. For some, death is the greatest healing—to return to the womb of the universe, having completed one round of the evolution of the Soul and come again into the embrace of the infinite.

We are desperate to feel that God is on our side. That "He" cares whether we live or die and that, like a loving parent, will grant our wishes. All of this stems from the terrible loneliness we feel here on earth, so apart from something we cannot even remember or describe. It is because we belong to the cosmos, and earthly consciousness is hardly a flicker of who we are. Our time in body is so short, and yet we do not remember ourselves apart from human form. The Soul inhabits the body during its incarnations; then is free again.

We pray to the lord of heaven to grant our prayers because we cannot imagine we have the power to change energy or our own reality—but we do! We have been shown how by many healers and saints, Jesus the Christ, and others who set the template for us, gave us their blessing and permission. Yet we hesitate because of the residue of unworthiness imprinted into our psyche from the beginning of our sojourn here on earth.

If we face death or destruction, a dying baby, a loss of fortune, we pray for the outcome we think is the best, never considering the hologram of a Soul and what it chooses to experience for growth. The baby that leaves its body may be offering a profound gift of love to its family who must search for meaning in this painful experience. Because we cannot hear the voice of its Soul, we cannot know what is best—spiritually. For us, it is a life cut short. For the Soul of the child, it may have been a brief encounter to pick up an evolutionary thread. The Soul holds a blueprint of evolutionary growth for its incarnation, but the choice of how its lessons are learned is a part of free will.

At the moment of conception, the imprints of the Emotional Body begin to influence the way we play them out. If our Akashic records hold memories of guilt or shame, we are more likely to learn those lessons through negativity because our emotional imprint is that we "need" to suffer to pay for our sins. We do not need to suffer, we need to expand our consciousness so we can see purpose and sculpt it from more joyful potential.

If we feel that God does not grant what we want when we pray, we say—"It was God's will." No, it is never God's will to hand us misfortune per se. It may be the hand of karma by which we grow in compassion and wisdom through experiencing the victim and the victimizer, but it is never to punish us and it does not come from "above," but rather from "within."

Imagine you are a conscious Soul who designs the blueprint of your incarnations so that you can evolve. The design is not about good or bad, but about growth. How you grow is a choice you make from the power of your free will, on the level of your Soul. There are infinite ways to arrive at enlightenment. Suffering is an outmoded psychogenetic habit that we must divest ourselves of at this juncture of our evolution. It actually blinds our illumination, and therefore our cosmic oneness.

The balancing of karmic acts from this lifetime, and any other, need not be put into perspective through pain and punishment. The concept of punishment and its personal relationship trappings come from the human mind. For eons we have been told that tragedy was the punishment of the gods, but it is not. Neither is it God's grace that saves us from misfortune or gives us that for which we pray.

If God neither punishes us nor saves us we might wonder: "What is God's purpose in our lives?" Perhaps it is merely to whisper to us our Divine Source so that we express its energy in such infinite variety that we evolve creation itself! We are here on a mission: to transform humanity into an ever more magnificent expression of Divine potential.

Our very evolution is threatened by the delusion of original sin and all of its dark implications, not because the masses think consciously about them, but because they have not been released from our spiritual DNA. We have entrapped ourselves in the religious quagmire implying that God does not want us to have infinite knowledge or power and that, in effect, we have no right to it. This is not true! To the contrary, our genetic encoding holds all the secrets of the cosmos. The universe exists within the matrix of our cellular database.

As we evolve we will let go of our need for personalizing God and grow into the consciousness of cosmic love, which is not about our everyday lives but about the wholeness of our being. We cannot relate to unconditional love, as yet, because we do not know how to connect through the Soul instead of the ego. Love without attachment is foreign to us because we have been hanging on from the moment of our conception, as if we have fallen into a deep precipice and will at any moment lose the foothold that could help us return upward. Is that a primordial, cellular imprint carried over from our decent down the fallopian tubes into the womb? Is it a spiritual memory that expresses the compression of a multidimensional Soul into a physical body—or perhaps, both?

One day we will free ourselves from fear and separation, banish illness and possibly even death through our own consciousness, and our prayers will become glorious exaltations to the Divine Source of which we are a part. As we evolve, we must change the essence of prayer to reflect a more holy communion than we do now.

We are taught to pray for our sins, for forgiveness, and for help. Supplication seems to be our primary theme of communication with the God Force. It is a form of bargaining, begging and pleading which confines us to realities of this dimension without acknowledging ourselves as part of infinite worlds of existence from which we can draw the wisdom to manifest for ourselves all that facilitates our growth. We ask God to do it for us because we feel helpless, unworthy, and entrapped in a physical world we cannot maneuver; and so we seek a miracle that must come from The Divine. Perhaps, above all, we pray for comfort. We long to be consoled for our loneliness and fear. Is it truly God that is comforting us when we pray, or is it that prayer itself comforts us?

Of course, it is comprehensible to pray for help when we feel helpless, but its motive is centered on the survival of the self, which is ultimately an impoverished view of universal truth. Perhaps we feel that when we pray for another, we are selfless, and therefore, deserving to be granted our wish. This is still the illusion of survival and not the honoring of each Soul's choice. When we pray for another, we must support their healing, liberation and joy within the context that they choose.

We pray in order to receive something we think we need as if God were some kind of supreme ruler who must give to us if only we ask. "Ask and you shall receive" is the biblical quote. Was the implication a kind of third dimensional gift contract? I think not. I am sure that the reference was about heavenly affairs. Ask to experience heaven, to be touched by the Divine Source, to connect to Divine knowing, to feel the unconditional cosmic love—yes!

How fantastic it would be to pray for illumination, for the strength to solve our problems, for the sense of oneness. Like preventative medicine, we could use prayer to focus our consciousness on the possible solutions that might come to us.

I remember seeing the Prayer of St. Francis on a church wall in Mexico many years ago. Although we attribute it to St. Francis of Assisi, we do not actually know who wrote it, but it is a template of enlightened prayer. It remains a point of focus for me and I have begun to use it when I perform marriages for couples who have oriented their relationship towards helping the world. Let me show it to you now as a perfect example of teaching ourselves to pray on a higher octave of consciousness:

Lord, make me the instrument of thy peace
Where there is hatred, let me sow love
Where there is injury, pardon
Where there is doubt, faith

Oh Divine master; grant that I may not so much
Seek to be consoled, as to console
To be understood, as to understand
To be loved as to love with all my soul

For it is in giving that we receive
It is in pardoning that we are pardoned
It is in dying to self that we are born to eternal life.

Prayer is a powerful tool to focus and amplify will. When we pray for peace or wellbeing, we actually conceive of that energy in such a way that it becomes a potential reality. Such prayers lift us up to an octave where we have the energy to bring them into fruition as a part of our purpose in life—the evolution of the Soul!

What would it be like to pray—**for** God?

Can you imagine what such a prayer would sound like, or its contents? A prayer for God would be a gesture without acquiescence, but with the aperture of universality. It would hold the knowing of potential and the grasp of infinite possibility.

"God, may you always evolve. May you create infinite form and variety throughout the eternal universes so that your Divine potential is expressed, and may we also evolve to be the true Divine examples of your creative force."

Now, could you take those words and extend them *energetically* to the Divine Source? In doing so, you would be completing an arc in concert with universal laws that what you extend out, comes back. The arc of energy would not be prayer as thought, but prayer as pure vibration. It would transmit a powerful signal of manifestation or creation back into the unmanifest universe of pure energy that could then concentrate the energy and direct it out once more in manifest form.

This is the stuff of miracles—only because we cannot see into the pregnant void of creation that holds all energetic potential. One day we will touch that void and come into perfect concert with the laws of the cosmos.

Eastern religions use the sound of (Aum) to come into the God vibration. It is a way of meditating on God without the chatter of the mind. By now it is recognized everywhere and heard in many gatherings of meditation, as well as a silent mantra for individual meditation. Aligning to this sound draws the consciousness into a Divine state of cosmic connection without the sense of above or below, or supplication. In actuality, this is our truest relationship with God. Why are we so afraid of it?

That which we can conceive, we know within our Soul. If we recognize the vibration of strength, then it is something we have inside us. Instead of praying for strength or love or courage, we might use our consciousness to find them within ourselves and wield them as Divine attributes in our lives. Instead of "Give me the strength," we could ask, "Where am I holding strength within my body?" Our body is of Divine creation, and therefore holds all spiritual and physical truths. If we are willing to seek our true selves, we will discover that the problem and the solution are linked through our own innate beingness.

The purpose of our presence in body is to bring new possibility and creativity to the One Soul through the experience of embodiment. Spiritual law holds that all endings are the source material of new beginnings—ad infinitum. If we understood this in our essence, we could truly "surrender" to the flow. The Soul is eternal. We will never be lost.

The conscious acts of devotion, prayer and meditation in which we engage are our external "doing" way of reminding ourselves that we are connected to the God Source. It is a purposeful act to sit in meditation, kneel in prayer, sing a song of God, and they all turn our attention inward to a place of harmony. We surround ourselves with images and other sensory associations that help us to remember the domain of The Divine.

Churches are replete with the paraphernalia of God. Because we do live in a third dimensional world, we have always used material representations to remind and focus our attention on The Divine. Every church uses symbology to communicate and imprint their creed of religion. This paraphernalia has even been repeated in variations from one kind of spiritual group to another down through the ages. In the same way that religious conquerors placed their temples or churches upon the holy ground of their vanquished, they also borrowed themes, symbols and cultural mythology so the conversion could occur more rapidly.

Many prayerful habits such as rosaries, malas, and prayer beads have been assimilated from one religion to another. They are all variations of the same theme allowing a person to run a continuous repetition of prayers through the mind while marking them on the beads that are passing through the fingers. Why do we place so much importance on the differences of our forms of devotional expression? Whether we cross ourselves left to right or right to left, as the Catholics and the Greek Orthodox do, or not at all for the Protestants, we have allowed these "signs" to amplify our differences, rather than enhance the acknowledgement of our collective love of the Divine Source.

The perpetual name-calling and derisiveness between religions must stop now. It is this kind of pointing the finger and blaming that sets the fires of violence and hatred. For the Christians to say it is the Muslims who are violent is so ludicrous that it is a glaring insult to the mind as well as the heart. History clearly shows how the Crusades and other Christian escapades epitomized the violent aggression in the name of the lord. Did the Muslims strike back? Yes, and it has been a three pronged trident between Judaism, Christianity, and Islam for too long.

Like petulant children, we have been striking out at each other for eons and finding all manner of excuses to destroy the preciousness of God-given life. We are **all** violent. Our religions are just the pretexts we use to justify our destructive urges, and our churches are all too often the breeding grounds for schooling hatred.

None of the founders of today's religions were violent in their initial intent. Every one of them lifted up from the desperation of daily life to receive new information that taught them peace, ecstatic joy and unconditional love. The tenants of their teachings were not even about how to live life, but rather they were apertures of consciousness into true source. How can we emulate them if we do not likewise rise up to higher levels of consciousness that can free us from the fray of struggle? We need our sacred places to set our frequencies onto a level to receive Divine energies.

What can we do to revamp our church going experience? Thus far, we have either moved to more fundamental, strict religious expression or we have tried to pretend that less "reverence" will make church more palpable. The new trend of making churchgoing "more joyful" is an illuminating commentary on our religious state of affairs. Churches are investing in drumming and other forms of enticement to attract people into religious service. All of this is mere cover up of the negative underlying messages bombarding us from the pulpits—"fear God and you might be saved."

There is a third and more true choice; it is to free ourselves from the stigma of past religious dominance and reinvent our relationship to a Divine Source that helps us access the meaning of our existence. Are we ready to forgo the cajoling of heaven and hell? Could we begin to experience Divine Source in the present, without the trappings of gender, martyrism, mythology or stories, rituals or symbols? Probably not yet, because all of these are intrinsically interwoven within our collective sense of self. However, we can begin to sincerely sift through them and see which ones can be released now and which can be expanded in new ways to make the God Force more a part of our lives. The church experience needs to become one free from obligation or guilt. It needs to become the profound celebration of our relationship to all we know as holy.

There are many churches and sects today that are focusing on the joy and celebration of the Divine Source during their devotional gatherings. Dancing, singing, and ecstatic states all bring the adherents into a more experiential relationship with their God—upholding the experience of God, not just the speaking of God. Silent meditation is another beautiful form of connection that frees the mind from its perpetual definitions and constructs, allowing cosmic truth to fill the void. Unfortunately, the underlying thoughtforms and imprints cannot be dissolved from the outside or from what we do; they must be released internally and consciously from our deepest psychogenetic encoding.

It is not the belief in God that needs to be undone, it is the antiquated interpretation of God that must now be left behind. Our belief systems urgently need to be revamped so that the enlightened core of spiritual understanding can become evident—for the first time in religious history.

What do all churches/religions have in common? The recognition of creative energies coalesced into what we call God or Divine Source. Mystics and theologians should embrace each other in acknowledgement that they both seek to touch and be touched by universal source. We can find the way to build upon this essential truth so that the awareness and honoring of any god form can be a point of commonality between all humans, rather than a destructive polarity. Churches today must not be bound to the stakes of past human servitude and suffering, but must break free in order to shine light on all Divine possibility that could illuminate evolutionary leaps of perception into the great mystery of humans and their gods.

EVOLUTION

1. Churches must begin to teach essential truths that are inclusive of all humanity.

2. Churches must revamp their teachings, dissolving control through fear, damnation and the residues of religious manipulation of the masses.

3. Churches can become the institutions of peace teachings across the world.

4. Sermons can become inspirational reminders of how to be of service to the world.

5. Churches can teach people to pray in new ways that activate the power of higher truth.

6. Churches can re-picture their beliefs through employing positive symbols and images.

7. Christian churches must remove the negative image of Christ on the cross.

EIGHT

GOD AND THE BOOK

WE HAVE CREATED A GOD OF WORDS, a god we describe through anecdotal conversations, stories of metaphor and hearsay. Our infinite possibility of knowing the God Source through our senses and consciousness has been eclipsed by the constrictive format of words that attempt to describe, but do not truly access the Divine vibration. The dull hum of time has translated mystical experiences and their subsequent illumination into the ambiguity of myth, cultural etiquette and mind. Millenniums of spiritual drought have left us only a dry seabed of murky residues.

Spiritual experiences have been covered in the sands of words that not only reconfigured them, but changed the landscape of universality as well, by rooting **individuals** as the trees of truth. Through the written context, historical episodes have taken on a life of their own that seem to erase the qualifications of validity from those who had the experiences, or told the stories, or wrote them down. The written words and mental pictures created an illusion of absolute truth, simply because they could be seen and survived the dusts of time in material form. Somehow the authors became the holy bearers of truth, rather than just someone who told the story from their own perspective or from that of whomever recounted it to them. In fact, were they not mere humans like you and me?

We too are available to feel Divine presence in any moment of our lives. If we wrote it down, might it not carry a seed into the distant future?

This idea that truth is cloistered in the form of words is with us today and will be, perhaps, tomorrow as well; we still believe the written word almost unequivocally. In ancient times, only an elite few had access to words in the written form. It is ludicrous to think that every word they wrote came from their own deep connection with spiritual essence. The scribes that recorded events did so at the command, and from the perspective, of their masters. Humanity in the past was as focused on gaining power and control of the masses as it is today. True spiritual intent on the part of the governing few was rare.

In light of the Crusades, holy wars and the survival realities of those times, it is safe to say that religion was often a weapon of personal gain. However, the written stories of those epic times tell us of the deepest human longing to be a part of something bigger than life, something that shows us our true potential, a path to walk that carries us on towards a life we have not yet known.

Stories about God are spellbinding, somber and mythical in scope. The magnificent writings set down in every religion to bridge the vast abyss between mere humans and their god are immeasurable treasures for all humankind, because of the window they provide us into the experiences and consciousness of our forefathers. Their spiritual experiences can help us to better understand ourselves and also to see how we have evolved. There is no religious text in existence that has not been "compiled" by more than one author over at least some span of time.

All of them began through the art of verbal storytelling and preservation through memory until ultimately each found a way to commit them to visual text.

The fact that those stories are stored in books such as the Torah, the Bible, Qur'an, the Vedas, Guru Granth Sahib and other religious texts gives finality to their teachings. Religious books are considered unquestionable points of spiritual reference and we have bestowed absolute authority upon their various authors who, in reality, simply were recounting events that most of them did not witness first hand. Yet they appear to be all we have of the origins of our faiths and that fact makes them, for some people, our most important link to Divine origin.

Even as new written Gospels are discovered, preserved in their original papyrus texts, some people try to ignore them because they change the contexts of the original stories. The newly discovered Gospels of Mary Magdalene and Judas tell very different tales of biblical events. That the teachings were to have been passed on by Mary Magdalene, who was painted as a whore, and Judas, who relates that Jesus asked him to betray him because he was the closest of his disciples, certainly bring into question the original saga of Jesus, claimed by all Christians as the foundation of their religious beliefs. Why are these new stories so devastating? It is Jesus, the great teacher of love, who should hold our faith together, not the circumstances of his life, which albeit are fascinating, but not the essential, powerful lessons he demonstrated and asked us to emulate and enact ourselves.

All of the sacred texts from the great religions speak with profound similarity about how to live life. Considering the often violent attempts by their adherents to say that they are polar opposites, they bear striking resemblance to each other as codes of conduct and templates of humanity.

The concept of the "Golden Rule" for example, appears in texts ranging from early Egyptian 1970 B.C.E., through Hinduism, Zoroastrianism, Taoism, Buddhism, Roman Paganism, and Native American Spirituality, among others. Imagine the Golden Rule as a teaching almost 4,000 years old, an idea passing through so many cultures, and yet we still have not learned how to live, "Do unto others as you would have them do unto you!"

Ultimately, only **we** can assess for ourselves whether we find holy books of Divine origin or not. They may be first person accounts—"God spoke to me thus…." or others recording a story told to them. The question of truth is not only about whether it happened or not, but also touches upon their subjective interpretation of God. Was it God in the burning bush, the angry god of Abraham, or a messenger from God? There will never be definite proof of such tales because they are the personal recounting of realities lost in time. We may find circumstantial evidence of a place or event, but that does not prove that God said it or did it. If only we could let go of our fixation on this point and focus instead on what those teachings mean to us today.

The difficulty lies in the question of their (texts) infallibility in terms of being edicts from the God Source. If they were, we must permit the possibility that they were given expressly to those living at that time, from a Divine energy that related to that era, rather than cling to the position that they were meant to encompass a stagnant eternity.

The Old Testament is filled with the slaughter of lambs and the demanded offering of gold and other precious objects to the "Lord." Perhaps this was the beginning of imprinting value on material things rather than the purity of the human heart. What would the lord do with such offerings if he were not in human form? If it were to show willingness to give up such things, it left the poor at a disadvantage to please, in equal terms, the almighty God. We now know that the Old Testament was composed over a period of time and that it never discloses its authors. It simply says, "God said..." But we must ask ourselves that dangerous question—"Who says he did?"

At some point we will have to enter into the conversation about "Who is God?" If in the end there truly is but one god, do we feel that the sun god Ra of the Egyptians was the same god of Abraham? Is the god of biblical times the same as now? Or is each god in turn, created by and for the consciousness of humans within their cultural realities? Evolution is a universal mandate. Thus, we must find the strength to perceive the Divine Source in new ways without fearing we will be lost in an eternal hell of separation from that Source simply because we have expanded our vision of God!

What we can do with the written texts is honor the wisdom our ancient religious books offer us, and at the same time, allow ourselves to pass through those parts that are so obviously inappropriate to our reality. If the old councils chose those specific texts, then perhaps it is past time for new councils to review and revise what we want to keep in them—for guidance, rather than sociological history or religious mandate.

The god of old may have said something to Abraham that was given to that moment and those people, which simply is not for us. In the same way a parent might give different mandates to children of different ages, it seems probable that over the millennia we have been shown truths that fit our level of comprehension at any specific moment.

All of the ancient texts from every religion are filled with ritualistic instructions and behavioral commands that cannot possibly be useful or even inspiring to us today. For example, the use of blood sacrifice and anointing with blood as a form of consecration for Aaron and his sons of the Old Testament smacks of a psychogenetic throwback to primordial times when symbolism was laden with gross density, and in which life was offered to bargain with and appease God. It is not for us!

Many interpretations of meaning would be altered if we read holy texts from a more symbolic or even historic point of view. We can easily intuit when something is symbolic or figurative as we are reading a sacred book. The images and meaning of messages that are not ours become warped as they funnel into our brain. It is as if only some part of the old brain can engage in its dull scope. Spiritual teachers who insist that every word of their books is that of God, deny the birthright of personal spiritual experience and intuitive knowing; they are frozen in the blinding dogma of religious storm. The heavy cloak of astral energy produced by old rituals from antiquity has smothered their clarity of discernment and rationality.

In many churches where readings from the Bible are offered as part of the program, the refrain after the reading is—"Word of God." In fact, they are readings *about* God or biblical stories, but very disputably, the word of God. The "word" of God as written, seems irrefutable for many believers worldwide. Those ancients who said they spoke to God or heard the word of God directly have given humanity a set of scenarios that millions have entrusted as absolute truth. For those believers, to question authenticity is the sin of heresy. Even to "broach" the concept of heresy for many of us is enough to activate negative psychogenetic imprints from the middle ages. Remember the five million burning "heretics?"

Perhaps those literalists fear that if any part of the written documents were found to be untrue, then the whole of their faith will crumble and fall, pitching them into a black hell without a reference point. It would be so much more palatable to acknowledge that some passages in all the major holy books have human infiltrations that we know are specific to their own time framework, and not of the highest spiritual content. Let us free ourselves from the mental chatter that blanks out the true revelations we seek.

What is indisputable in terms of religious texts is that **men** copied down stories and conversations of their own, and from hearsay, many times, hundreds of years after they occurred. The infiltration of cultural cues is palpable in them all. The very stern voice of Abraham's angry god is nothing like the gentle voice of Jesus, whose loving manner bequests a new view of the God Source.

It is mystifying to me that the possibility of personality infiltrations seems so threatening or that any variation of image is labeled heretical, since those variations and interpretations are absolutely intrinsic to the shadowed creation of the original documents. If we cannot allow the probability of a certain amount of human and cultural filter through which religious texts passed in order to be recorded, then we are eluding our true knowing. The mandates and messages were all sent **through** people.

Sometimes the words of the Divine Source were said to have been given by angels or other intermediaries. Yet, again, that information comes from a being who had a subjective experience of spiritual origin. How could they have understood a message that did not reference their own cultural, reality framework? Contemplate for a moment how easy it is to interpret what someone says by what you "feel" is true. Imagine what might have actually been transmitted and yet not understood or recorded!

Every time a text was translated, it had to pass through the accepted code of the day. Many words in translation took on nuances that changed their meaning and interpretation of the author's intent. The translators themselves were bound by their own religious training as to how they interpreted the meaning of a word. We have seen a great deal of confusion and entered into endless debate as to the meaning of statements that have been translated into different languages that can only approximate the original transmission, which was itself a subjective rendering.

The word "sin" for example, in its original meaning referred to energy out of balance, not an act against God; witness how prominent that word has became as a weapon of unworthiness and disapproval. These twists have brought darkness and pain to the connection between ourselves and the Divine Source that should have been one of absolute joyful reverence. Did God make it a hellish relationship? No, that was man's own creation. If we ask why, we will be thrust into the realities of power and illusion, manipulation, and control of the masses.

Today, archeologists and other scientists are uncovering information that sometimes verifies and sometimes debunks religious doctrine. It is thrilling to hear that we might have found Babylon or remnants of the Ark, or newly uncovered scrolls. These findings lend support to the historical stories of the Bible and other religious texts, but they do not prove that God said or commanded this or that, nor do they confirm that God is actually the being presented to our imaginations by those who struggled to relate to a higher power through their limited personifications thousands of years ago.

The hope that such discoveries confirm God, stems from our desperate longing to validate our own existence and purpose. If God exists, then so do we. But of course! Could we also say that since we exist, so does God? Our perpetual problem is that we cannot envision anything but a homogeneous God of our own likeness—how limited, how quaint!

We do not have to take everything as absolute. Why do we care so much if our sacred books are literal truth? Are we so mental that we cannot utilize the allegories, the symbolism, and the creative poetry in them as valid ways of touching The Divine? For me, it is fascinating just to perceive how our forefathers interpreted the Divine force because it tells me about who they were and how we are different today. Some of their experiences are profoundly inspiring in that they demonstrate the possibilities for us to feel Divine presence or witness miracles. Could we imagine ourselves being healed by the essence of love and encouraged to do the same for others? Yes, absolutely!

The famous question, "Is the Bible truly the word of God?" should not be the cause of the hostility it provokes between those who believe ardently that it is, and those who see it more as a historical, sociological, or inspirational book. The conundrum of whether it is, or not, may one day prove to be irrelevant, because we are experiencing the cosmic push of evolution that brings us to today.

How can we accept only those texts from thousands of years ago as the true voice of God? In every era there are multitudinous people who feel that the Divine Source speaks to them. Why would we not believe that present day conversations or teachings are possible? If it were not possible, then we would have to conclude that our greatest fears of being alone, abandoned by God, have come true and that somehow we are inferior to, or less worthy than our forefathers. These conclusions simply are not valid.

I feel that some of the tenacity about the Holy Bible as "word of God" stems from the desperate need to think of God in a personal way. We don't seem to care if that personal relationship has been constructed within the confines of fear and punishment. We actually allow ourselves to think that God is waiting for us to make a mistake so we can be punished in hell, rather than think we are free to create our own heaven or hell. Without the imprint that God is watching, listening and judging us, many people would not be so focused on the shadow of hell, nor be as compliant to their religions.

The teachings of the Bible are given through its allegories about life and the consequences of how we live it. Some of its proposals positively do not fit the world of today. In Exodus 35:2 it is written that God tells Moses, "Whosoever doeth work on the Sabbath therein shall be put to death." I don't think anyone today would follow that edict. How could we hold that God said we should put someone to death because of a default in time? Do we not think it is even better to worship God every day of our lives? There are many such mandates in all holy books that we cannot take literally because they are in direct opposition to other mandates in those same books, or are contrary to what we now hold as rules of humanity. How does killing for God fit with the commandment, "Thou shall not kill?"

The second commandment states that the lord god is a jealous god. Jealousy is not a level of Divine understanding that is instructional to humanity. To the contrary, it has caused infinite suffering and confusion. Further, the voice of God purportedly said that in punishment for any digression, he would cause suffering to one's children's children, unto the third and fourth generation—hardly the tactics of a loving and confident lord! Though in olden times it was common to scar future generations through the actions of their forefathers, today we would consider that to be unethical and inhumane.

Is it all or nothing? Do we feel that we must accept carte blanche every word of those ancient conversations? Biblical scholars will not enter into such arguments, because the contradictions are so blatant. They will engage endlessly in intellectual arguments about the meaning of certain texts, almost as if to distract themselves from the questions that any small child would ask, "Why is God so angry?" Many people have told me that they never really believed the stories about punishment and sin, that they always knew it was just adults attempting to control them. How brilliant and clear are the children!

Judaism, Christianity and Islam alike, embrace at least parts of the same holy texts: The Torah, The Old Testament and The Quar'an, respectively. Unknown scribes compiled these books over extensive periods of time. They are filled with the historic sagas of the peoples of that era—their battles, their bloodlines, their mandates to please their "Lord God."

The biblical prophecy that the Jews were the chosen ones, but would travel the world without a home and be hated by all others has been a self-fulfilling prophecy. Because of the self-hatred and hunger to override his own secret background, a little man named Hitler turned a colossal campaign against his own demons into an astral monster that almost swallowed up a culture of people. We cannot let this happen again—ever!

The Old Testament says that God told Moses this and that, "and God said to Moses—," but we never know upon whose word this is so; the speaker is not identified. There is absolutely no proof that the lord of biblical times spoke those words.

Perhaps it is not the "proof" that counts, but rather the value of the message—not the messenger— that makes a difference. Certainly we feel that a message about unconditional love or compassion is more powerful if it comes from our god, but in truth, the actual power of it comes from its essence. The lord of the Torah, the Quar'an, and the Old Testament offered mercy in exchange for loyalty. "If you do this, I will do that; or if you do not, then I shall cause the other." This kind of "buying and selling" is not a template for spiritual enlightenment, much less a design for conscious living, but it does illuminate the motivations that brought response those thousands of years ago—and perhaps it is true today, as well. Let us hope we still respond to fear mongering in the same way because of our psychogenetic inheritance, which can be released—rather than as an indication of our true nature.

I think we are still caught in the shadow of those stern methods of forcing obedience and it seems as if that lord's followers today perpetually use the same techniques of fear and punishment to ensure loyalty. Other Divine models, such as Jesus the Christ and the Buddha, never found it necessary to engage in such negative patterns.

Could it be possible that the lord of those times might have evolved because humans themselves have lifted up to higher energetic levels, and yet we hold him back in that place of anger and will, because that is how we were introduced to him through our religious books? Fear dies slowly.

The three major holy books share in common the story of Moses, and how he conversed with God and received the first Ten Commandments. While the Ten Commandments certainly gave us guideposts for living a righteous life, they hold some negative aspects that bind them to an old time reference. Most of them are given in the negative, which entraps us in the fear and judgment so prominent from early times. "Thou shalt not" sets the dynamic of polarity and separation. Perhaps this is why it is so much easier to find fault in others rather than see the good in them. We have laid down in our psychogenetic encoding what is "bad," but we have not really imprinted what is "good." If we were to change the emphasis to the positive, we might live a more enlightened reality.

The Jewish Torah honors the Ten Commandments as the most important behavioral rules in the Hebrew scriptures. The commandments do not, however, address many of the moral issues of our times. To the contrary, they mention instructions that are not considered ethical to us: death as a punishment—while contradicting it with the commandment, "Thou shall not kill," "manservants" or slaves, negative references to women, jealousy and even Divine favoritism. Today, we ponder the morality of "prochoice," euthanasia and other themes of free will and self-determinism that are not illuminated in the Ten Commandments.

Since we are all created from Divine spark, the truth of our divinity is indisputable. Thousands of years ago we could not grasp the magnitude of such a concept because we did not have the conscious perspective we have now. Though we can stretch our minds beyond molecules and subatomic particles, we still have not given ourselves permission to see God beyond our human repertoire, and so we cling to our human point of reference.

Is it possible that all along we were accessing an intuitive truth that the lord we have embraced is a local kind of god that has dominion over our earth or galaxy? Perhaps there are layers of Divine consciousness, which will come into view as we expand. This need not neutralize our belief in one god, but rather allow our awareness to engage the many facets of such luminescence that are beyond our present intelligence.

Today, having traveled to the moon and beyond, we could include ourselves in a larger hologram and conceive of a universal Soul.

Through that source of infinite truth, we could create new mandates—commandments for ourselves that would integrate a higher humanity and help us to truly be a part of the vast universe. If we have evolved over the last several thousand years, we might be able to access the "God within" that allows us to perceive ourselves from a much different octave of innate goodness and bright potential.

Imagine yourself as an enlightened being who could direct the actions of humans. What kind of commandment would you give? I have written a few, just for the exercise of speaking about what I think is essential to our human family. If we mastered these points, all the other conversations of fidelity, stealing, and coveting would become things of the past. I know there will come a time when we will have advanced enough so that all laws of action and beingness will come directly from within. Here are the ones that came to me. I hope you will spend a moment accessing your own.

1. Always embrace your divinity and in all ways live divinely. Speak and act as if you were the Divine Source. You are your Higher Self, the all-knowing, intuitive essence of your Soul.
2. Witness the sacredness of life. See it in all beings. Know that there is Divine purpose in each experience and in each life.
3. Bring Divine consciousness into every aspect of your life. Wield your business, your body, and creative endeavors all from the spin point of your Soul.
4. For all things, be grateful. True gratitude for all experience and all people, ultimately brings enlightened evolution.

5. Use your body as a Divine vehicle. Learn to commune with it and it will bring you health, ecstasy and illumination.

6. Entrain your mind to find possibility and potential in every dilemma. Your own Divine Source gives you access to all solutions.

7. Always speak your truth from clarity and compassion, and give yourself permission to change that truth as you grow.

8. Whatever you want, give that. If you want love, give love. If you want money, give money. If you want acknowledgement, give acknowledgement. It is the giver who creates.

9. Balance the male and female energies within you so that each has powerful, yet gentle expression.

10. Teach your consciousness to hold goodness and inspiration.

The Bible does offer beautiful parables of inspiration. I am not referring to those of martyrs and victims, but stories of people helping people, of healing and performing miracles. Jesus the Christ urged us to do all that he did and more! We think this is impossible, but it is not. Once a template is created, it has an energy that can be activated. Wouldn't you like to heal the sick, feed the multitudes with a loaf of bread? The images created by these texts are indelibly inscribed in our psychogenetic framework, and if we choose, will surface in the moment we say yes to them. I think that moment is now.

Many people are unaware that the contents of the New Testament were also chosen by a select religious group who "decided" which of the testaments served the church best. The Council of

Carthage in 393 C.E. anchored in the structure and beliefs of the modern church, which has changed little from that time.

Unknown quantities of scriptures were weeded out because their tenets did not uphold the views of the governing body. Reincarnation, for example, is said to have been sacked because the poor proclaimed that they would pay their taxes in the next life. Too many religious decisions have been based on economical or political expediency, rather than any deeper belief system or spiritual mastery. Since the world has always been moved by such key forces, we can understand how this came to be. However, when we see that other versions of truth or history alter what we have held as truth, we must find the courage to move forward into a more enlightened awareness of The Divine, and for the sake of the future, change what needs to be changed!

There are gospels by Mary Magdalene and Judas, as well as others—that were not chosen. We can easily guess why. By the time the church came into being, there was a specific story about Jesus the Christ that formed the basis of the Catholic church. Any information that changed that story was, and still is, vigorously suppressed. The focus on his suffering and death on the cross was a powerful instrument for bending people to the will of the authorities. Are we still at this level?

Why do we cling to this kind of negative rigidity? Would not any new information enrich and enlighten our lives? Wouldn't it be better to free Mary Magdalene of the whore's yoke, in effect, placed upon her by those early priests who wanted to reduce the power of female priestesses; or even better, free ourselves from the judgment placed upon those who are caught in such an existence? Do we really need a traitor to blame in all scenes of trial and tribulation? To redeem Judas from his treacherous role might change our own patterns of betrayal. If Judas were asked by Jesus to catalyze his capture, as he claims in the Gospel of Judas, it could mean that Jesus had a plan all along and was not the victim we think him to be. It seems that his whole fiasco on the cross must have meant something more than the redemption of humans, who as fledgling creations, need evolution— not redemption!

If a group of religious leaders got together today to create a modern sacred text, would they choose the same Gospels or include others? Is it possible that today God's edicts would be different? Would they be commandments, or might they be teachings that help us to perform miracles, or bring our awareness onto the plains of cosmic laws, or perhaps open us to the sensations of infinite love? Would our religious leaders dare make such changes? Do they have reference to these higher energies and knowings themselves?

In the United States we founded a nation upon religious freedom because our forefathers had carried the brunt of religious oppression and conformity at the will of others. One of our presidents, Thomas Jefferson, actually re-created his own Bible! The Jefferson Bible: "The Life and Morals of Jesus of Nazareth," was his thesis on how Jesus' teachings were incomplete and subsequently impregnated with additional grafts planted by the disciples whom Jefferson referred to as Jesus' biographers, and later, the evangelicals. Considering himself a clear-headed rationalist, he took it upon himself to cut out the references from the New Testament he found suspect of antidotal untruths. He extracted only those teachings and stories from the New Testament he found worthy of Jesus, whom he saw as the greatest and purest "god being." Can you imagine a president who dared to imply that we needed to review something so old and sacred as biblical scriptures? How very inspiring and courageous!

What do **YOU** want to believe? There are beautiful stories of inspiration that can take us out of the darkness, and there are untold tales that are happening now, which could help us to touch the Divine Source. What would be the most exalted kind of story for you? Would it be one of inner peace, or unconditional love, or miraculous experiences with the Divine Source?

The Holy Qur'an speaks of action in faith. One of the most beautiful examples of this is the "call to prayer." Every Muslim is required to kneel in the direction of Mecca 5 times a day and say his prayers. In predominantly Muslim countries, even commerce is interrupted. Western countries might find this a bit impractical, but the concept of bringing God into the forefront of your life several times a day is nothing short of awe-inspiring!

Unlike Christians and others, the prayers of the Muslims focus on the honoring of Allah's mercy and greatness, rather than the supplication for things we want or even what we think we need—"Give us this day our daily bread..." The Muslim call to prayer speaks of Allah, the one and only God; the surrendering to his greatness, and the recognition of Muhammad, his prophet.

Spiritual action does not need to be only within the visible or material realms, as in recital of prayers. It could be purely the focus of consciousness that perceives the Divine energy around us all and embraces, or even directs that Divinity into our world. Muhammad, like Jesus and Buddha, was a channel of higher wisdom offered to an unenlightened world.

The incongruence occurs because the ongoing recitations from the Holy Qur'an are often about fear of God and his retribution to those who do not comply with his mandates, as well as the consequences for non-believers. The style of delivery is inordinately similar to that given to Moses, though the focus is on the recitation and memorization of the message. To recite the threat of punishment does not uplift or enlighten the spirit, but poisons it into a state of impassioned numbness.

The story of Muhammad meditating in a cave and finding his connection with God is beautiful and inspiring. The way he described the sensations that came to him tell me his experience was of the highest order. At first he heard the sounds of reverberating bells that gradually congealed into the voice of the angel Gabriel. Gabriel insisted Muhammad recite what he passed to him as the words of Allah, which were later written down. Like those delivered through the Ten Commandments, the messages were about how to surrender to the infinite power of Allah, the one God, and how to live the way he prescribed.

Muhammad ultimately transmitted mandates that served his culture during the time of his life. Those mandates were, however, filled with the separation between human and Divine, and offered up war and punishment as the only resolution to the battle over God's power and truth, just as did the Old Testament. If Gabriel told all these things to Muhammad, he may have said them on his own and his role as intermediary seems blemished by his actions of the time. Allah the merciful could have spoken directly to his messenger without Gabriel's filter. Are angels so perfected as to truly be echoes of the lord? I think not.

It is said that Gabriel named Muhammad as the only prophet to carry on into the future. Gabriel's pronouncement must leave us to wonder at the timelessness of the astral dimension—"Muhammad is the last prophet—he is the seal of prophets. No legitimate prophets will succeed him," is the decree of Islam. How could this be? Has the god of the Jews, the Christians, and the Muslims forsaken them? If ever we need new prophets, it is now. Why would we presume that any new teachings from Allah would defrock those of Muhammad? They could simply be a new wave of enlightened life.

How could it be that God would send no word to us in the last several thousand years, nor in times such as these? Could time and evolution stand still? How can we say that new prophets with great wisdom will not arise—and that we should not allow them? Why would there be no new instructions on life or even more important—new glimpses into the Divine cosmos? Is there really no new truth to inspire our lives?

I do not believe it could be about our unworthiness. Perhaps it is because the laws of energy state that the answer lies innately within the question. In other words, we are the solution to our dilemmas and until we recognize this, we will not evolve to the next level. I would answer to myself that despite the arguing, memorizing, recitation and transcriptions of holy texts, we still have not managed to ascertain their true meaning. We fight about whether they should be embraced literally, figuratively, symbolically, or not at all.

What has struck me in reading sacred texts of the major religions is the violence that is sanctioned within them. Is the reason for this that the tribes of those times were focused on conquering and war for mundane power and survival? As surely as the sun rises, new Divine prophets have now, and will, come to us—within and beyond our established religions. Will we kill each other and our precious children as the price paid for new ways of perceiving universal truths— "The Evolution of God," or will we make the leap to entirely new realities?

What is true is that we have not found the way through our **minds** to integrate such great illuminations into our lives. Instead, we have manipulated them down into the smallness of human expediency, and thus diluted their energy so as to not be comprehensible at all. It is not ethical, nor enlightened, to kill each other in God's name.

Perhaps a better way out of the "God wars" is to find experiences and knowings that free us from the enigma of religious words. It is the translation from holographic Divine energy down through cultural guideposts, past intellectual and intuitive limitations, and into human reference points that cause the terrible wobble of hopeful truth.

Muhammad was a gentle, loving being who helped everyone around him, and yet in the end, he led his followers into war against the Arabs, his own culture—in the name of God. It was the only choice he felt he had, and he was sure that Allah would support him and smite his enemies. It seems that each new religious awakening has always been met with violent resistance and accompanied by bloodshed.

In today's world, we do not need teachings of war; we need examples of peace to lead us through a questionable future teetering on the precipice because of the human habit of fighting. Religious fanatics of all faiths are egging each other into battle so they can prove who is the beloved of God. "Allah the Merciful" is reduced to an empty expression when religious fanatics cut off the ears, hands, and feet of offenders without so much as a backward glance at "mercy" as a Divine mandate. There must be a better way, a new way!

I am not inspired by the admonitions of old! I am not fearful of God's wrath, nor am I fooled by the religious mandates for gaining heaven or avoiding hell. "First there was the word" and as we embraced it, it seeded itself within our minds. Was that word "God?" Did we imbue it with primordial fear? Is it really true that humans respond best to threats of punishment? It isn't that I don't think such negative energies exist. I know they do exist because we have created them as part of our religious repertoire. We needn't have gone in the direction of darkness, and it is now time to correct our course.

Let us not pass on this negative potential to our children's children. What would happen if, like Jefferson, or even the religious authorities of old, we edited religious texts to contain only the most uplifting and holy of messages? Let us extract the best of our holy books and our religions so our lives can come to a new octave that will instill future generations with all the beautiful attributes of our humanity.

I believe in the goodness of humans! Why is it that with all the messages of the sacred books, we cannot seem to live them—

that we cannot find their goodness? We study the words, but they are frozen in mental levels of existence. I am sure all of us feel we do good things sometimes. Why not actively practice that goodness, rather than just talking about it, or using it to convince ourselves we are enacting the words of these holy teachings?

The Divine long existed before someone said the word God or wrote it down. To clutch the Bible or any religious text as the gateway to God seems flat, as if we humans only touch with our minds. Given all our senses, mere thought—though powerful to set references—can never take us through to the other side of consciousness where we might "know" God in essence.

All religions began through the Divine inspiration of their founders who were somehow thrust across the veil into realms of pure energy that took them out of their human arena into one of cosmic proportion. Religions cannot be based on writings alone. They must carry with them a sense of awe and essence that goes far beyond words. If we hold on to the words, we will ultimately find ourselves empty and without the Divine connection that is essential to life. Up until now, we have been imprisoned in the word stage of spiritual understanding rather than the stage of deeds, or even beingness.

May the books of our spiritual source teach us beyond thought—to essence, to conscious awareness within the great, infinite formless universe. Humans are preparing to call the cosmos home, to travel into the void and return with the knowing that brings each of us into the Divine fold.

All the sacred books have helped our fledgling species of humans find a way to live, to develop cultures, and to discover our cosmic source. Now it is time for us to access the Divine messages that carry us beyond laws of life, on to laws of Divine energy. We must learn how to become enlightened beings who can manifest and wield energy without suffering.

We must lift the teachings from their encapsulations and practice them as something real, as if they were steps in a dance. Then there would be no fighting, no lonely separation. I could do the dance of true Muslims—surrender and mercy—or the steps of the Buddhists—compassion and peace; the Hindu AUM—God within; the Native American—the spirit of all things; or the Christian—unconditional love—couldn't you?

In the end, our spiritual evolution is not what is written in a book, and it is not even what is said, nor who said it. Rather it is how we take a message or teaching that inspires us, that allows us to feel our connection to The Divine, and how we bring that into our lives, becoming what we truly are—beings of Divine Source. We have had the force of thousands of years abdicating our direct experience of that Divine Source to the religious leaders who are deemed worthy, because they have spent an allotted measure of time studying God. It is our turn to touch directly, to experience for ourselves, that which could never be encapsulated in the flatness of a page or the confines of a word.

My loving heart pleads, "Come beyond your books—come into the heart of humanity where God truly dwells. If you touch that place, you will become the truest essence of all you have ever read."

EVOLUTION

1. Let us sift through the warnings and fear inducing messages of our holy books, and dissolve their content so that our consciousness embraces the true kernels of spiritual wisdom, which can guide us into the future.

2. May we reach through the pages of our holy books into the essence of the Divine Source, and experience it directly through our own awareness.

3. Let us practice divinity though the examples in the books of how to live compassionate, loving, truthful, and inspired lives.

NINE

WOMEN AND THE DIVINE

THE HISTORY OF RELIGIOUS EVOLUTION has almost entirely occulted the feminine aspects of communing with God. The story of women and The Divine is as convoluted as human history itself. Female spiritual linage is filled with whole epics of visible, then invisible participation in our relationship to the God Force. From the early virginal sacrifices, to the power of the prophetess and seer, to the spiritual voice, the Goddess, and lastly, the delegated source of original sin, women have been eclipsed and then stepped forward time and again. As we shake ourselves free from the illusion of God in the form of a human male, we will finally allow everyone to express their sacred divinity without the shackles of gender.

Virtually all early religions saw the female as sacred, even as the most venerable to be sacrificed to the gods because of their mysterious Divine energy of procreation. Worshiping the Goddess became the format of daily life hundreds of thousands of years B.C.E., and the fertility goddesses took their place as the most crucial gift of tribal survival—they were equally as powerful as any male gods and at some point superseded them.

In the time of the Goddess, it was the women who created the vision of divinity and were the source of spiritual expression. They wielded the power to connect with the gods, and nature was the focal point of worship. Spiritual activities were about maintaining balance with "Gaia." The clairvoyant, intuitive and listening powers of the priestesses were honed to communion with all living creatures, as well as the natural symbolism of the planets and the elements of the earth. The seasons were marked with ceremony, and the power of birth was the great mystery that was celebrated by all.

The Eastern religions that worshiped many gods embraced female goddesses as part of the hologram. There were goddesses who embodied the Divine feminine and brought nurturing, healing gifts to humans, while others were feminine in body but as violent or war-like as the male gods. All of them were honored and brought into the daily lives of those who worshiped them. Egyptians, Romans and Greeks all had pantheons of goddesses to whom they turned for guidance on the crucial matters of their lives.

The Oracle of Delphi was visited by nobles and leaders from distant lands as well as the simple people who sought out the priestesses for clarity as to whether to wage war, or plant crops, or who to marry. Each prophecy was given in such a way as to insist that the recipient interpret its meaning himself. This kind of encouragement to find truth within the self is the highest form of illumination, which we so need to practice today.

It is a gift of feminine consciousness to allow growth, rather than choose its particulars and force them upon another. From wherever the goddesses came, they sought to enlighten humans and improve life on earth rather than the emphasis on themselves and what they demanded of us, unlike the male god who has been interpreted by the yang energies to be an angry, punishing god. The feminine god energy opens the threshold into the unmanifest worlds beyond human reality and bestows the gift of creation upon the evolving beings of all dimensions. It is the absolute source of the unmanifest void and returns there without the kind of bondage the masculine God Force engenders.

Only a few Goddess names have been passed down to us. While Divine templates in the masculine remain, the feminine have disappeared. Is that because of the God wars, or is it because the Goddess energy left us to move through these stages of evolution on our own? Is it possible that the spiritual qualities of the feminine allowed their bearers to return to higher octaves or dimensions of light, while the heavier structured male energies are still bound to earth through karmic ties that keep them in human context until they have rebalanced their energies?

Why did the Goddess era end? The power of the Goddess influenced the status of all women and in many societies women held title to land, which was passed down matriarchal lines to daughters—a thorn that ultimately became a wedge between the male/female relationships and played a part in the usurpation of female power by priests. (Amongst the rhetoric of religious justification for battle in God's name, we always seem to uncover a monetary motive lurking behind the noise of righteousness.)

As early as the second millennium B.C.E., a pronounced struggle erupted between the adherents of monotheism, the one male God, and the pagan Goddess worshipers in the biblical areas of the Middle East. The Levite priests of Canaan took up the fight to take back the power from the female and her monetary might by stripping women of their rights as priestesses and reducing them to the inconsequential roles of servants to husbands and fathers.

As monotheism took the stage, the religions that honored female goddesses were either snuffed out or left to areas of the world not considered a threat to the conquering religious hoards. It is not surprising that THE God, the only God, male in gender, was imbued with the forceful and demanding attributes that men claimed to follow.

Since men could not replicate the sacred and mystical act of giving birth, they had to find a way to diminish its relevance to the God Force. Perhaps the fear of that exclusively female domain triggered the priests to focus on erasing the feminine power. It is also likely that the lingering ostracism of single females today is a carry over from this period when they embodied a mystique of dangerous potential.

The seeds of jealousy had been sown and the intent to destroy the influence of the goddesses was set in motion. Aided by the story of Eve's wickedness, the priests justified their attacks on women, and the temples of goddesses were taken down, their sacred texts destroyed, and the Divine wisdom of the feminine god, lost to humanity. What could have been written in those texts? From that point on, women were not allowed to participate in rituals with the men, and in most cases, not at all. The capacity to even write or record was lost to women as they were excluded from the power of education.

We must now recognize that the portrayal of The Divine in male form began in historical times with the sole proposition of territorial and temporal dominion. The priestesses were destroyed along with their profound spiritual wisdom; erased from all potential reference that would guide us today merely because of political and religious expediency. We are still entrapped in the illusion that "might makes right;" however, amidst the techno thunder of the present, it is almost comical to think that physical dominance is the criteria for truth—yet in those times, physicality ruled destiny.

From the sacrificial offering, to the form of the sacred Goddess, and ultimately to the displaced outcast, women accepted their defiled place with no audible argument. Why? Perhaps in a world of overt physicality, they simply did not conceive that they could use their more subtle attributes to change the balance in such a violent atmosphere. As Christianity swept the world, it emphasized the story of Eve and her evil, seductive powers that were the cause of "original sin" and the downfall of humanity. How easy it was to fit the blame of misery into the gentle body of the female!

As a consequence of the violent holy wars, inquisitions, and other male dominated religious activities of early times, women were forced to hide their natural powers of healing and intuition. Without their intuitive sense, women lost their awareness of Divine body and Soul. The female role became of little consequence and women quickly forgot themselves. As time passed, the priests grew heady with the possibilities of power over their societies and they began to subjugate women more and more severely. They invented the concept of the virginal wife and the uncleanness of women because of their menstruation. These judgments have only been neutralized within the last century, and certainly not in all societies.

Knights and Christian soldiers of God often "deposited" their wives into the confines of monasteries for safekeeping. This protection had more to do with guarding their ownership of wives and daughters than with God. The austerity of such realities was thrust upon women, who effectively had no say in the affairs of either politics or God. Imagine the constriction of a chastity belt or the walls of a monastery! Motives for the monasterial life were as much for hiding as they were for penance or God's grace.

The Bible states that God created Man in his own image. The insistence on literal interpretation has created such polarity as to alienate us all from each other. We might pause here to wonder what the Bible and other sacred books would contain if they had been written by women? It is certain that there would be a different and more generous approach to men than has been shown to women, and perhaps life itself. It may be that more Gospels, such as the Gospel of Mary Magdalene, will surface and illuminate female consciousness as it existed in those ancient times—before and after biblical reference.

Where are the scrolls and tablets from early Samaria, Egypt, Greece, or India that could bring forth the voices of female prophets and bearers of the Sacred Feminine? Were they all destroyed with the temples? We can be certain that they did exist. However, let us not fall prey to the illusion that what is written is "truth," or that texts from the past constitute proof or bestow value upon the protagonists of the tales. We women are Divine, godly and powerful with or without intellectual acknowledgement or applause—we are only now on the verge of this great rebirth of feminine consciousness.

If the Bible were specifically speaking about the male gender, rather than humanity in general, it could be implying that men were to be seen as the favorites and highest of God's creations. While we might presume it meant both male and female, there is a glaring difference between the female form and a male god. There is no question in my mind that men in antiquity created God in their image so they could relate to such an incomprehensible energy through the blinders of their conceptual faculties.

This image conversation runs amuck for women because we would already be in a second position with God, as our female bodies do not conform. Certainly, that is the way men have perceived the story from the beginning—i.e., a male god instructing the course of humanity, through men! Witnessing the male interpretation, it seems as if they were the older siblings suffering from the disease of painful jealousy, attempting to dismiss and diminish their competing sisters.

The female body is not a mirror image of a male God. To see the human form in generality without gender reference simply delays the inevitable conflict of scriptural aspersions about our female sexual energy. If God holds a male form, then women are different from God and will always relate through some kind of gender polarity. We either project the father energy onto God, through which we see ourselves as the helpless and weak children, or we are perceived as holding the covert thread of male/female current whereby we want to attract God for primordial, pro-creational purposes.

This later potential has cast a shadow upon our inherent spiritual power and lurks in the crevices of all church doctrine.

In fact, the Divine Source laid the survival and future of our species within the maternal womb of the female—plain and simple. Only women can give birth—how interesting! Certainly this must signal to us the obvious truth that women are Divine in essence, and godly in form.

Intrinsic to this power, the Goddess religions embraced sexuality as a part of honoring the Divine Source. The undeniable sexual potential simply cannot be extracted from the female equation; and it seems ludicrous that we would attempt to peel off aspects of our humanness and convince ourselves that some parts of us are what God created and some parts of us, just somehow, occurred by themselves. Sexual energy is a part of who we are; part and parcel of the human genome. The godly gift of sexuality is still in its cocoon of potential and awaits our awareness of self beyond the physical body. In the end, we will discover that form does not refer to only an outer crust, but rather is a term referencing a holographic template. We will ultimately be enlightened by the fact that "God" may be much more than the human male we have come to expect!

It is very hard for us to consider releasing the mythology of the father because of our lack of historical awareness, our own sense that we could not possibly have the answers or be the heroes ourselves. We have become attached to the father figure as a teacher, as a god who will take us through the steps, who will show us how to come to a new level of our being. All of us long for the mentor, the teacher, the father, the God, and we don't realize that all around us are those energies in many forms. Not only in the masculine form—the God—but in the nurturing form of a mother Goddess, or even in the gentleness of an animal.

All humans remember the warmth and safety of the womb and through our psychogenetic inheritance, hold within us the essence of mothering. The energy of mothering is sacred because it nurtures the Divine ovum and brings it into the world, growing it into the future generation. I predict that we will eventually abandon the masculine, tyrannical godhead and come to embrace the Divine mothering principle that provides all we need to become our greatest potential—and that we will find it within ourselves.

In today's world, as more men from many cultures begin to be present at the birth of their children, even aiding their wives, there is a profound enhancement of the union between them. How incongruent it is to be side by side at the sacred moment of birth, and yet not be allowed to embrace our Divine Source as equals. In diverse cultures and religious practices, women and men sit segregated from each other because of this underlying sense that they would be distracted from worship in each other's presence. This gives pause to contemplate whether cultural laws and taboos arise from religious thoughtforms, or the other way around? In any case, it is fair to say that they function because of collective convenience, not universal truth.

It seems obvious to me that the whole statute of men and God, and women and God, being two different conversations, is a fabrication of the exclusively male religious domain of our forefathers. Virtually all monotheistic religions have cast sexuality into the abyss of sin against God, or at least spun a thick web of taboos around it, subtly entrapping women in its midst. Most of our lack of honoring the Sacred Feminine comes from the biblical imprints about Eve that have overshadowed the Divine Mother role in creation.

The book of Genesis portrays Eve as the seductress and the source of all the evil that resulted in our fall from God's grace, and the expulsion from the Garden of Eden. The implication is that she was more aware, curious, and powerful than Adam, and that he was so inherently weak he could not resist her calculated seduction to join her in an unauthorized adventure whose consequences were grave—that he was, in fact, the victim of her power.

Perceiving the creation myth from this perspective, we can comprehend why the fathers of faith have worked so hard to trounce upon the all-pervasive power of the feminine, fearing that women are still following in Eve's footsteps and leading men away from God (and the church). Even more probable is their fear that the Sacred Feminine would one day return and dissolve the false foundation of masculine religion.

The female has always represented the un-manifest knowing of mystical worlds. It is evident that the outer needs the inner, and that both male and female hold each of these qualities within their essence. I find it fascinating that religious truths are often brought forth through feminine, yin channels of gentle wisdom, and then forced upon the world by excessive masculine, yang conclaves intent on destroying anyone who does not bend to their way.

Such is the story of Jesus the Christ who embodied a male form and yet brought forth the wisdom of the loving feminine. He took to his side Mary Magdalene, whose fate in the hands of history has been violent and unjust—perhaps because she was his truest disciple or because she represented the powerful Goddess energy that needed to be destroyed lest it inspire others to follow her.

It is not enough for me that we "believe" the early church turned Mary Magdalene into a whore, how they used her to dissolve any possible power of the feminine force within the church, or as a part of the god conversation. It is not enough to expose the absurdity that women are too impure to enter into a house of God, that they should sit only amongst themselves, or that they cannot guide or express religious thought. It is time to expose these manipulative tactics and rebalance our spiritual direction. These are all the societal politics of God from many religions and cultures, and they are untrue.

What is coming to light about Mary Magdalene and her star role in the life of Jesus the Christ is breathtaking to consider and may well turn the tide towards the Sacred Feminine once more. Not only may she have been his "wife," but she may also have been his most powerful disciple. The discoveries of the Dead Sea Scrolls offer evidence that Jesus may have planned for **her** to be the leader of his new faith. It is entirely possible that she was very much part of the great teachings on compassion and unconditional love. Many people have experienced lifetimes within the body and consciousness of Jesus. The overwhelming majority of them saw Mary Magdalene as the one who rolled away the tombstone. What does this mean? Possibly, she was not a simple woman, but rather another great being of otherworldly powers!

Ultimately, we must ask ourselves whether those supposed biblical scenes in which Jesus saved her from being stoned were about sexuality, or for some other political intention. I would question whether they are even remotely true. Who wrote that story? —A man. Although, I very much like the teaching—"Whosoever is without sin, cast the first stone." It is a sentiment that would serve us well today and it encompasses a whole treatise on judgment, which would help us to realign with the teachings of compassion and truth that Jesus taught.

The Christian church might find it unthinkable to contemplate that Jesus **chose** to be crucified, or that he was healed in the cave and then came again to the world in his true Christed identity—but this seems completely logical to me. If he raised others from the dead, why would he not do the same for himself—especially if that were actually the point in the first place? It is time for Christians to turn the proverbial page and see the life of Jesus from the magnificent reference of a Divine being who came into human form to bring the truth about embodiment and its potential!

The new theories that Mary Magdalene may have born Jesus a child fracture the old stigma of divinity in opposition to human sexuality. The most intriguing aspect of this scenario is the sexual bonding with Mary Magdalene that produced a child. If we can entertain this possibility, the entire history of sexual meaning will have to be undone! Not only would we find a new meaning of sexual and spiritual communion, but we would be able to free ourselves from the prison of such a dense illusion as to who we are and the powers we have to participate in our journey of evolution.

What happens to you when you hear about the idea of Mary Magdalene having Jesus' child? Does it frighten you to consider that we women had a play in the sacred—outside of the dubious honor of being sacrificed? Is your first thought—sacrilege? There is such a deeply held psychogenetic imprint that embodiment is not holy, that to couple sexual union with divinity seems truly heretical. It is not!

The Catholic church has allowed and even advanced the cult of the Virgin Mary (mother of God) because her asexual identity offers no threat to the main thrust of Christianity—that Christ was born of a virgin through immaculate conception, died for our sins, and ascended to heaven. Mary Magdalene represents a frightening challenge because she is a partner, a vessel of the Sacred Feminine, and even the most dangerous of all—a flesh and blood template of Divine Mother through her female body.

However, Mary Magdalene's conception of a child is not nearly as interesting to me as that there is some evidence intimating she produced a **girl**! Sarah. The miracles performed by Jesus showed him to have profound power over life and death. He must have "chosen" to bring a girl into the world. This is exciting to contemplate. Why did he want a girl? In a world today, where many women feel that their fathers would have preferred them to be a boy, what was Jesus thinking? Was he again showing us an evolutionary direction, giving us a teaching of unconditional love, of the power of feminine spirituality? Was he offering a lineage of feminine spiritual energy to carry into the future?

In biblical stories and in many religions, women have been the "handmaidens" of God. Forever, we have been the holders of light and truth from the time of temples. Often we were the symbols of purity for priests who were seen to be the direct representatives of God. In a way, women have always been the seers and men the seekers! What they saw and what they knew has been lost to us; and yet we can intuit that there was, and is, a great deal of spiritual clarity and truth that rests in the feminine. Perhaps it is our time to bring it forth again, and that is why we were born women.

How, then, could it be that we women have to fight for a place in the religious arena? Even on mundane levels we have been labeled unclean, dangerous, and therefore forced to comply with commands of where we can sit, what we can wear and how we are to comport ourselves. In early times, women were commanded to cover their hair in order to show respect and diminish the blatant truth of their femininity. This façade of respect is a way of forcing women to cower in the inconsequential corner of servitude.

Catholic women around the world still wear mantillas on their heads in church and Muslim women wear the higab or headscarf. The higab has created such emotional and social uproar that it demonstrates the degree to which we see each other from external, rather than deeply human perspectives. In some parts of the world, Muslim women have lost their jobs because they choose to wear the higab as a sign of their faith or cultural sense of propriety. Non-Muslims are disturbed by this glaring demonstration of polarity, as if the knowledge of one's religion could create an actual threat! No one would demand that those who wear crucifixes should remove them because they excite a religious confrontation, yet that sight might trigger ancient fears and hatreds on the part of Muslims whose forefathers suffered the brunt of Christian furor.

We in America cherish religious freedom and recognize that the motive for outer religious expressions is not to excite the wrath or fear of others, but rather it is about ourselves. Each and every one of us has the right to embrace our religion in all aspects of our life. What is this fear mongering conversation really about? The saddest part may be that women look at each other from a place of expectation to be ridiculed or judged, coming from both sides.

We women must seek the place of peace and convergence because a majority of the males on this planet seem to struggle with the idea that we can live peacefully as humans, or that we have a mutual destiny. It is time that both women and men who hold the psychogenetic inheritance of intuitive and loving spiritual essence, step forward and awaken to the reality that we must learn to trust and honor each other. Our cultural realities have eclipsed our essential humanity—one Soul family that has come to earth to transcend and evolve.

Why do women continue to be shunned in the religious arena? Pope John Paul II declared in 1994 that the church has no "authority" to allow women priests. In light of the fact that Jesus and his disciples invited women into the fold and utilized them as missionaries and teachers of his message, it seems a ruse to pretend there is no precedent for women clergy. Now that Episcopalians and most other Christian churches do allow women, the Catholic church again finds itself outside the kind of modernization necessary to sustain itself.

How different would it be if the world saw God as androgynous or as God the mother instead of God the father? I would suspect that religion would be quite different, but these are all perspectives that are a part of our human conversation—not that of our Souls. Feminine, or yin energy has always been an energy of inclusion that reaches out and brings all potential together into a cohesive whole. That is why it is so necessary to bring feminine energy back into the conclave of religion at this time. In action it connects the visible and invisible worlds, and thus completes the circle of spiritual energies. Neither side of the equation seems appropriate in and of itself. We are designed to compliment each other, and the exclusion of either only creates the kind of imbalances we have endured throughout the centuries.

Although I am profoundly grateful to be a woman in this lifetime and feel the Divine grace and clarity it offers us all, I find myself un-intrigued by burgeoning Goddess cults. The rituals and rites of the past take us back into the astral stickum of that past and tether us to energies that are not conducive to our highest good today. Women engaging in such activities may not recognize those astral energies, because their outer awareness is focused on the celebration of life in the moment. There are thoughtforms and karmic lessons that are still caught in the cellular memory of ancient times, which are not supportive to our present consciousness. They could include manipulation of nature, power struggles, and initiations so stringent as to include death. These are repetitive themes that do not advance our spiritual evolution.

We need to bring all of the magic into our common domain within the routine of our everyday realities. There are many mysterious points of mastery that we can call upon without the kind of manipulation that often occurred in the past. Certainly the communion with nature, the gift of creation and the awareness of our place in the natural world are attributes that we could bring with us. The power of birthing can be translated into many aspects of life. We are not bound to use birth through our bodies, but we are beginning to see that birth and mothering offer great wisdom. If we do not give birth to children, we must wield this spiritual potential to create in art, ideas, cultures, etc., so that this Sacred Feminine energy passes through the vehicle of our presence, a more subtle aspect of our body.

In effect, it is the Sacred Feminine, rather than the Goddess that we need to evoke now. It is time to depersonalize The Divine and ourselves so that we can forge the ego into an energy of oneness. In this pivotal moment of earth's history, we do need to call forth all our capacities to listen to the messages of other dimensions, but it is not necessary for us to sequester ourselves away from the world, nor do we need to proclaim ourselves the queens or priestesses of the natural or spiritual worlds.

All of us, men and women alike, have psychogenetically inherited from the goddesses the undeniable power of feminine knowing, intuition, and clairvoyance. We need to live the wisdom we have inherited within our spiritual DNA so that we can open onto a cosmic universe beyond such minuscule details as we perceive in this moment. We can do this, even now—but we must do it through the eyes of the feminine essence that know the way across the veil into the infinite un-manifest.

I predict that it will be women who will bring new spiritual realities into form in the near future and that they will not be anchored in the flatness of words or the dryness of dogma, but rather they will be seeded in the unfaltering wisdom of the heart. Let the women come forward and open the threshold to the center of the Soul!

The world as we know it is about to have a seismic shakeup so intense as to make all of these heady deliberations of the past completely archaic. We are on the brink of discoveries that will carry us out into the universe. Our explorations will completely change our view of God!

EVOLUTION

1. Check to see if you hold any negative thoughts about women as unworthy to be sacred beings.

2. Look for any subtle thoughtforms that women cannot be the priests, preachers of God, and release them. (See Chapter 12, *Technology of Consciousness*.)

3. Release any/all condescending judgments of the goddesses.

4. Contemplate the feminine attributes of your spirituality and how they are expressed in your life.

5. Meditate on the mothering principle at your core, and allow that to extend and merge with the Divine Source.

TEN

GOD AND SEXUALITY

NOTHING SEPARATES US FASTER from the sense of sacredness than the conversation of sexuality! The very word "sex" has been marked as the antitheses of God for so long that even though we ostensibly do not believe this, we harbor its poisonous residue deep within our psychogenetic encoding. Sexual energetics have been blamed for almost every deception between humans and God.

Religions have adamantly refused to look at the connection between our conception and the beautiful forerunner to it. Since many religions support the negative concept of original sin, even the miracle of birth bares the tarnish of something not acceptable to God. How incomprehensible to see the perfection of a newborn baby and swallow the dogma that it is born in sin—especially for those religions that do not embrace reincarnation and think this child has only one life in which, before even beginning—birth has placed the baby in a state of sin! Why did we do this to ourselves? Such destructive interpretations of life simply are not worthy of our power of reason today. When will we learn to trust our own knowing and to rid ourselves of such implausible concepts?

It would seem obvious that the Divine energy allowing us to procreate could only be "God given" as its mysteries initiating life are beyond us. We can grow life and even create clones, but we cannot "initiate" life. Therefore, sexual energy, the vehicle of conception, must be connected to our spiritual source and moves in tandem with creation.

Why have we separated our sexual currents from our spiritual ones? In so doing, we have cut ourselves off from the one-ness and beauty that come from the sacred linking of the two energies. One of the most positive aspects of ancient God-dess spirituality was the universal sense of awe and mystery that surrounded the sexual act and everything connected to it. The priestesses of the Mother Goddess embraced sexuality as Divine, and utilized its power as the foundation of life and the harmonic pulse of nature. If only we had kept their wis-dom, our sexual experiences might be a joyous celebration of creative potential and an avenue to spiritual experience.

Sexuality is not only about reproduction, it is about the merg-ing of polarities that makes it part of our sacred human experi-ence. We bring Divine energy into our bodies when we make love and bridge the gap between human and Divine. How did we lose this higher application of our sexual reality?

Most likely, it was when the Levite priests took the power from the priestesses that our negative interpretation of sexuality was initiated as a part of the plan to discredit them. Moses was of the Levite lineage and may have participated in the over-powering of the priestesses in the very lands where matriarchal, goddess societies had guided humanity. Wielding the graphic tale of Adam and Eve and their shameful expulsion from the Garden of Eden, the priests imprinted the multitudes with the fearful correlation between sex and punishment. Sexuality became the scapegoat for loathing the female and even the mystery of reproduction. After the downfall of the priestesses, the emphasis on sexuality as a natural part of life was erased and replaced by a stern and foreboding God.

In the time after Christ, Christians believed that Christ would return to "judge the living and the dead" at any moment— Armageddon was neigh! Because the "second coming" of Christ was imminent, the priests discouraged sexual activities in order to pass the scrutiny of Judgment Day and avoid entrapment in hell—celibacy seemed the best protection. How quickly Jesus' loving principles were forgotten and the more malleable, negative threats of punishment put into place to control the masses. Thus, celibacy became the call of the priests, and the taint of sexual contact, the sin of the multitudes.

It is interesting to note that today's culture reacts in just the opposite way to mortal danger. As if there were no tomorrow, people feel free to try to squeeze life into this moment and reach for the most thrilling sensations they can grasp, i.e., sex. Are they not afraid of hell? Is it that the sexual urge wins out, or is it that we really don't believe anymore that sex is a sin? Are we not tired of the religious rampages against something that is so intrinsic to our human reality? Above all, the idea that Jesus would return to judge us is not plausible—even in the face of biblical quotes, because he preached against judgment his whole life. Hopefully, the teachings of love and tolerance brought to us by Jesus are beginning to take hold.

Jesus was a Jew. Jewish Mores in those times did not allow an adult male to be unmarried and it was unheard of that such a thing would happen. There is absolutely no documentation that shows Jesus to have preached about celibacy as an access to God's favor. To the contrary, it seems unlikely that his teachings on love would have excluded the primary human relationship. Sexual love is a part of the union between a man and a woman, and since Jesus may have walked the earth in such a way, it is not impossible that this was part of his own human experience. He never spoke against sex. He only spoke of love. It has been said that he frequently kissed Mary Magdalene on the mouth, much to the consternation of several of his disciples, especially Peter! Why? It is likely that Peter was jealous of Jesus' devotion to Mary Magdalene and felt some insecurity over whether Jesus would choose Mary Magdalene to lead the disciples and his new church.

If further evidence finally proves that Jesus and Mary Magdalene were a pair, then the entire foundation of Christian sexual negativity will have cracked open and we will be free to embrace our innate sexual energy as something that is truly Divine in nature! The fear of Christian faith is that if Jesus were married, it would prove him mortal. Is there no way our minds can stretch enough to see that both could be true? Jesus could have been a mortal prophet as well as a Divine voice—a master of energetic laws, a cosmic being of godly proportion.

Mortality and divinity are not mutually exclusive—except to the narrowness of linear thought. It has been said in all great religious texts, "Life brings death and death brings life onto ever new octaves of cosmic consciousness!" Whether Jesus died and resurrected himself onto a higher plain of existence in Light Body does not depend on whether he was a sexual being or created children. We are lost in this confusion only because we have not understood that all humans are a part of what we call God!

If we could grasp this concept of being part of God energetically, we would live as so many ancient masters did—filled with light, on a plain of absolute abundance and love. Sexuality is only one gift of godly manifestation!

However, early Christian priests believed that Jesus had been an asexual model of a life worthy of the lord. It seems plausible that the story of Jesus' life was molded into the tale of the savior, untarnished by women or original sin, fulfilling the prophecies passed down through the ages to fit into the confines of church theology. If this were the case, the Crusaders and other "defenders" of the faith did an almost perfect job of erasing any reference of Jesus as a mere mortal. As they scourged the land, destroying precious artifacts and documents, their shadow swallowed untold references as to the truth of his life.

That the early clergy began to despise sexuality is completely understandable. If there is something we fear or that is prohibited to us, we must find a way to not want it, to convince ourselves we don't need it and that it is "bad." My Higher Self taught me, "Whatever you resist, that's what you get." It seems the same was true for the unfortunate priests who tried to resist and found that the temptation and fantasy of sex only grew on them. Imagine such an outlandish technique as to keep a young woman in the priestly abode in order to strengthen resistance to such temptation. In a world without the vast communication network we have today, many a priest could assuage his guilt with any number of excuses that only he would hold in his mind, without scrutiny from the outside governing body of the church. It is this undertone of evil and forbidden pleasure that has brought sexuality down to the levels of perversion and imbalance so common today.

The pros and cons of celibacy went on from around the fourth century until ultimately, sexual indiscretions became too troublesome for the church to handle, and thus the law of celibacy came into being. Celibacy finally won out, not because it was a mandate from God, but because it was a choice that the church made on its own and for reasons that may actually have had little to do with spiritual law. One fascinating conclusion was purportedly that if a priest engaged in sex, he would not pay attention to God! I must smile to think that we cannot see the Divine Source outside of our own time zone. Would a true God be angry if a priest spent time in relationship? What is human time within the great cosmic sea?

In good faith, we presume that all spiritual leaders are committed to devout focus on their godly pursuits. The thoughtform behind the idea of dangerous distraction is that women and God are in competition with each other. Is there not the possible truth that a couple can use their union to truly amplify their spiritual connection to The Divine? Of Course!

Apparently, the religious leaders had no faith in the loyalty or integrity of their brethren. Another covert reason for the celibacy vow was that "classified" information about the innermost workings of the church was leaked through lovers; and thereby sex became unconscionable.

The Catholic church did not actually ban priests from sexual contact until the 12th century, and only after many variations on permissible behavior. The first Pope was the disciple Peter, a married man. It is said that his wife, Perpetua, joined him in preaching and even performed baptisms. We could therefore call her a priest in every right, as well. The Bible describes Peter as Christ's choice to be the first head of his new church—where then do we surmise celibacy as anything more than a dogmatic policy decision created by a collective body, long after Christ made his intentions clear?

Martin Luther, the founder of the Lutheran Church said that it was this restrictive religious interpretation that most aided him to sequester followers into his reform church. He chose to permit marriage for his clergymen and many other reform churches followed suit.

Celibacy has been embraced to varying degrees by many religious seekers. The Hindus, Buddhists, Taoists and others have sought a path to the Divine Source unhindered by worldly realities; each with their own specific energetic perspectives. They may speak of celibacy as purity and grace, but unlike Christians, most refrain from the angle of sin and punishment as an argument in its favor, and yet again claim celibacy is necessary in order to give one's self to God. The mandate for humanity at this time is to bring the Divine Source "into" daily life, rather than to shun that life and return to the isolation of the caves.

The celibate Catholic clergy have had to perennially defend their position against priestly sexuality in a world that has grown tired and mistrusting of such loosely formulated arguments. In light of the increasing awareness of sexually abused children at the hands of confused priests, there is a rising swell of discontent in such a restrictive papal mandate. This critical moment truly demands that the church respond relevantly to the realities of the day, but instead, it insists on making the dangerous choice of hanging on to perspectives that do not serve itself or its followers.

The Catholic church's problem of sexual abuse could be helped tremendously by allowing the sanctimony of marriage to be given priests or by ordaining female priests. I suspect that somewhere in the dark unspeakable depths of the church's psyche lies the fearful residues of some sexual current between women and God, left over from the destruction of the Goddess cultures and the convenience of "evil" Eve.

The Catholic insistence on the "immaculate conception" creates an interesting whisper about leaving out the carnal aspects of life and separating sexuality from all that is good or holy. It is the kind of purity that helped to separate Jesus from human contamination. The virgin birth as an alternative, is much more palatable and safer to a religion that abhors even the fantasy of a touch between someone Divine and a mere human.

It is fascinating to realize that the story of the "immaculate conception" is a part of several mythologies belonging to ancient times, and thus may have actually been borrowed by Christianity, rather than the idea that Mary's immaculate conception of Jesus was the only one. The magic of such a phenomenon is not about its opposite, sexual conception, but rather a mystical act of its own. Why is it that we must conclude if something is good, its opposite must be bad?

It is time we changed our obsolete views of sexuality so that our religious awareness can truly enter into the world in which we live. The Divine Source could only intend sexual ecstasy since it is part of our genetic encoding that facilitates expression of our spiritual inheritance within the physical realms, as well as all the others.

However, the power of sex has had such a formidable effect on people that virtually all religions have codes of ethics regarding sexuality—with whom, when, how it can take place, and the sanctions and taboos that surround it. It is universally perceived as a force that must be controlled and met with the fierce hand of religious authority.

There have always been laws pertaining to the safeguarding of the genetic pool so that healthy offspring were produced. The sexual taboo against brother and sister, and first cousins relates to the weakening of the bloodlines as a result of too close proximity. We have witnessed the result of this genetic danger in kingdoms and isolated communities where it occurred because of lack of suitable, or even political choices. However, barring the advent of children, the love of someone so close in terms of blood is entirely comprehensible. Almost everyone can relate a story of falling in love as children with either a cousin or sibling.

The taboos concerning the "how" of the sexual act are likewise concisely relevant to natural law. The orifices of the body are governed by the direction of energy. For example the mouth takes energy in to nourish the body and at the lower end, the rectum expels unwanted energy. To force anything up the rectum is against the flow of bodily energy and eventually leads to imbalance. The act of sodomy or anal sex is solidly outside the wisdom of bodily energetics. For the love and safeguarding of one's body, it must not be done.

I am often asked questions about whether a predilection of one kind or another is good or bad. I feel that the categories of such polarities are old, limited ways of viewing truth. Homosexuality, bisexuality, etc., are not outside the scheme of natural law, except perhaps, within the form of lovemaking. My Higher Self says that it is not to "whom" you make love that is important, but it is "how" you make love. By this it means that sexual energies need to flow through all the energetic pathways of the body, not just the genital area.

We imbalance our whole beingness when we have sex for reasons of release, for power, or out of loneliness, thereby holding the energies only within the genital level. The profound and orgasmic rush of sexual union wants to rise upward through the solar plexus, heart, and on to the higher realms of consciousness in the head. When it does this, the whole body is nourished and is opened to spiritual octaves of oneness. Falling short of its true destination, it becomes an energy drain that affects the subtle emotional and spiritual bodies, as well as the physical body.

Sexual "orientation" is just that. It is affected by a multitude of factors. Since we carry the genetic encoding of both father and mother, we are all male and female, with the entirety of their repertoire. We must look at what that means in terms of the expression of those two opposite perspectives. In other words, the male inheritance for both males and females will be attracted to its opposite female counterpart. This is part of the explanation for why we seek those of the same sex as ourselves. Each child is attracted to the parent of its same sex because of the reflection of his or her own body. What I am saying to you is that because of this dual inheritance, we are all bisexual in subtle ways. If sexuality were not so frightening, we would be able to utilize these forces energetically, rather than as mere physical potential.

Our own bodies give us the best feedback as to how to proceed sexually, what is in balance and what is not. If we seek the advise of our bodies, they will quickly tell us how to make love, when and with whom. There is a powerful and palpable energy that moves between two people when their bodies "fit" together as sexual, emotional and spiritual compatibles. We have not learned yet to listen well to our bodies in these ways—but we can learn.

Many religions make sexual contact before marriage or outside of marriage a sin. These taboos have useful societal purposes, but they are not spiritual law. Marriage itself is an institutionalized societal conformity, and sexual attraction is a powerful force that brings us to marriage. If we have this resonance, we feel that we can face our future together. Although there is a beautiful sentiment of "saving" sexual exchange until after marriage because of its sacred nature, it is rare in today's world. In fact, the sacredness of sexuality is always true, with or without outside approval. Sexual embrace carries with it the potential for spiritual union in and of itself—unscripted by religious sanctimony.

There are a growing number of religious groups that create ceremonies in which fathers promise to encourage and protect their daughter's virginity by showering special rewards and acknowledgement upon them. The daughters pledge to their fathers to remain virgins until marriage. Sometimes they are given virginity rings. This smacks of "daddy's girl" playing she is her mother, and is probably not healthy in multitudinous ways. Having dealt with many women who cannot truly give themselves sexually to their partners because they are unconsciously bound to their fathers, I question the wisdom of such

THE EVOLUTION OF GOD

contracts. Many young women fail at this and thus compound their guilt about sexuality and diminish their self-esteem. This is all too reminiscent of medieval times and begs to uncover unconscious imprints and motives of the fathers.

In reality, there is no going back to times when women were virgins entering marriage, or any other of the rules that were set out to curb sexual interplay. The accepted double standard of taking only a pure virginal bride was certainly as much about male ego and political concerns, as about purity itself.

Affairs and extramarital sexual activities were banned from before biblical times, and for good reason. Participating in dividing two married people holds a strong negative karma and sex outside of marriage is hurtful to the union of the two partners. In the 1960's when we tried to loosen the chains of sexual guilt by defying the Mores and the entire concept of sexual evil, we not only broke the ties with tradition, but for many it was the thread of their connection to the church that was broken. How can one who practices free love go to church each week and listen to the ranting about the evils of sex; or enter the confessional only to once again confess to sexual behavior even after last week doing penance for it?

Since our religious authorities have not been able to live their own standards as regards sexual conduct, we have also thought it okay to pretend one thing and do another ourselves.

The "free-love" generations opened up whole societies to a clearing of concepts that needed revising, but not necessarily for the right reasons, or without consequences. One thing that became obvious was that sex for sex's sake, left deep grooves of pain and loneliness underneath the bravado of sexual independence. Though many people learned to disengage or block emotional feelings from the sexual act and to pursue it from a strictly pleasure seeking motive, they often found themselves left with a new kind of emptiness. Because of its affect on our entire beingness, sexual energy needs to be mixed with both emotional and spiritual frequencies in order to bring to fruition its powerful potential—without the unbalancing wobble it otherwise creates.

You cannot engage in sex without emotional content unless you close your solar plexus/stomach area, which is the physiological center of the Emotional Body, in order to protect yourself from connecting with your partner. This actually shuts off vital energy circuits throughout the body and causes negative reactions—depression, sadness, self-judgment, and emptiness.

Sexual currents naturally rise up in energetic passageways through the solar plexus, heart area and into the higher centers. Stop and think a moment. You know what that feeling is like. It is that tingly sensation that opens your whole body, melting fear and separation. You forget the need to protect yourself from intimacy and, for a moment, you feel a profound oneness. If you can go that far, you can heighten your sexual experience enough so that it brings you into ecstatic states that are truly spiritual in nature!

It seems necessary to understand sexuality from a more holographic perspective than just its enactment. Sexuality is a multifaceted energy, and its pleasure, drive and power over us are sustained by our Primordial and Emotional subtle bodies. The Primordial Body is the force of procreation that understands no limit of age or generation. It recognizes all sexual nuances as potential enactments of procreation and even beyond possible impregnation, longs for the union of our most essential elements of yin and yang.

The Emotional Body has access to cellular memories and functions through association and conclusion. It may be inexplicably sexually attracted to someone and lead us into all manner of entanglements through its feelings of deep and powerful connections. Since it cannot decipher the source of those feelings, it presumes a sexual bond, because that is the strongest energy it recognizes.

The connection may actually be a cross reference to emotional feelings for one's parent that occurred from conception or in the early stages of life when the child first becomes aware of sexual energies. That same energy is then projected onto the person because of some subtle gesture or similarity that causes an association to the parent and childhood memories. The most probable connection is a multi-incarnational memory in which we recognize someone with whom we have deep karma. They may have been a lover or spouse then, and unconsciously we attempt to replay that memory packet with them. These psychogenetic memories arise from our emotional and spiritual DNA and are not dislodged easily, even when divorce or disharmony will be the result.

Master spiritual seekers throughout centuries have practiced sexual/spiritual techniques without lifting the Emotional Body into the higher frequencies necessary to withstand or sustain these energies in body. Denying their emotional energetics may have helped them attain a certain degree of enlightened detachment, but the result was a person cut off from life at its full human level. This may have been their intent in the first place, but the purpose of life in our time is to bring the higher energies into body, not remove one's self from life. The Emotional Body is capable of higher frequencies and we must nurture and train it to bring our connection to the Divine Source through octaves of ecstasy, rapture, and bliss. All three emotional, sexual and spiritual components allow the perfect mix for a kind of sexuality that has not yet been utilized as the uniquely human attribute that it is.

Our entire conversation about sexuality begs a higher understanding on all levels. It is important to explore sexuality in its entirety as an energetic that has purpose on physical, emotional, and spiritual levels. Each of these sexual levels interfaces with the rest. I speak of sexuality as a current of energy that moves throughout all levels of the body and its subtle counterparts. Because it is an inherent aspect of the life force of the body, it is present from birth to death, whether we are conscious of it, approve of it, or not.

Children have these electrical currents diffused throughout their whole bodies until the master glands begin to message activation of certain hormones at puberty wherein the energy begins to focus within the gonads or sexual organs. After puberty the erratic sexual currents create profound disturbances in the physical, emotional and spiritual bodies.

The word sex for most people describes only one aspect of sexuality that refers to engaging in sexual conduct—through the genital area. It is truly an illusion to think that one can "have sex" with someone-else as casually as having a cup of tea with no further repercussions than a moment of release or satisfaction. This level of sex is so basic as to not represent much more than limited creature comforts.

Because sexual energy is the vehicle of potential embodiment, it is not a one dimensional frequency, but rather an intricate weaving of physical, emotional and spiritual energies. In fact, a "one night stand" will leave energetic traces for up to nine months. The two energy fields (auric fields) of the partners will be intertwined for at least forty-eight hours. The emotional currents will intermingle as well as a host of subtle biochemical energetics, even if they feel no real emotions for each other. Whatever emotions are stored in their emotional repertoire can be transferred to the other. If either partner has an ongoing or brief sexual relationship with a third party, those energies will also be mixed into the pot!

We have no defenses to block the energies of sexual partners or blood relatives. What does this mean? It means that we become each other to a certain extent. This is the reason that many people feel strange, tired or confused after sex. Recognizing this, it is easy to see why people attach those feelings to shame and guilt. They are exposed to energies that are not inherently theirs. The immediate experience may fade from their consciousness, but their body will hold the energetic signature for quite awhile. Extramarital affairs are covert only because we do not want to face what we already know is true.

It seems that we are now in a place of understanding the human body enough to be able to move with the flow of sexual energy in such a way that it fulfills all its potential. Are we now ready to explore its spiritual components? Though there are faint traces of sexual/spiritual understanding, they have been muted for thousands of years.

Eastern masters teach how to take the pure kundalini (cosmic life force energy) from its place in the lower energy centers at the base of the spine and direct it up the body to the higher centers of consciousness in the head. This effectively bypasses the purely sexual activity of the genital organs themselves. Several religions also aim to bypass sexual interplay by prohibiting their priests or monks to have sexual contact with anyone. What a profound difference between the two as the first harmonizes the sexual current and all its potential with higher energies, while the other suppresses all recognition of it in abstinence and opposition to the Divine relationship they both seek.

There is still a third sexual possibility that focuses the sexual act on the conversation of The Divine. It is called Tantra. Tantra is a revelation that began thousands of years ago in India. It embraced the wisdom of the body as a vehicle to attain Divine enlightenment. The forms and followers of Tantra are as varied as its practices of mental and physical sexual discipline. Tantra honors the Sacred Feminine much like the goddesses of old, and in most practices, that honoring includes the sexual act as the threshold into Divine spaces.

Tantra has been dismissed by many as a misuse of sexual energies degraded by blatant pretext of spirituality, while in fact the actions of the adherents are simply promiscuous sex. However, anyone who studies the concept of Tantra will be inspired to lift his or her sexual energies onto a higher octave. Tantric wisdom is truly profound within its art of weaving sexual physicality into the infinite web of Divine spirituality.

As the two intermix, we bring the God Force more directly within human realms, and our own conscious awareness is lifted up to meet the cosmos in such a way as to help us see that we belong there.

These all-embracing octaves of ecstatic bliss could lead you to what I call "cosmic orgasm." The orgasmic rapture goes beyond any normal bodily perception and does not even call for a partner or sexual activity. It is the kind of experience that changes all the sexual impulses for a lifetime.

Let us begin a new era of sexual expression in which we are truly ourselves—without the play of guilt or fear or shame. Let us be conscious that our sexual energy is mysterious and Divine and that these qualities can be mixed into the experience of it in the physical so that through sexual expression, we are transformed. Let us make love with delicious joy, with all our hearts, and for the purpose of oneness. Let us once again use our sexual energies as an avenue to the Divine Source!

EVOLUTION

1. Contemplate your deeper fears about sexuality and God. Release them from your body. (See Chapter 12, *Technology of Consciousness.)*

2. Become aware of by whom and when you were taught negative imprints about sexuality.

3. Identify your thoughtforms and release those you truly know are not true. (See Chapter 12, *Technology of Consciousness.*)

4. Practice becoming aware of your sexual currents and feel them awakening your heart and higher consciousness.

5. Practice perceiving your sexual partner as a Divine, spiritual partner.

6. Allow the sexual act to open you to oneness of spirit, and extend that to experience it as oneness with the cosmos. Cosmic orgasm is available to us all.

7. Imagine your sexual energies carrying you into realms of bliss in which you are a part of the Divine Source.

PART THREE

The Potential

ELEVEN

TRACKING YOUR OWN
SPIRITUAL REPERTOIRE

TRACKING YOUR OWN SPIRITUAL REPERTOIRE will be a fascinating exploration of your spiritual roots and help you to see many aspects of your familial and cultural self that you may not have been aware of. In doing this, you will open new avenues of spiritual conversation within yourself and also with your relatives. You will be helping everyone around you through this process. As you talk to the members of your family, you will be truly amazed about their religious concepts and feelings. If you approach it with an inquiring, "listening" mind, without reproach or intellectual argument, it may open up a whole new kind of communication that will illuminate a deeper conclave of your true feelings and how you came to be who you are.

The purpose of this is not to find fault with your family, or culture, or religion, but to help you see what you want to choose and what you want to release in terms of your own spiritual values. As you spend time with them in these conversations, you will begin to detect the difference between what they have psychogenetically inherited or been taught and their own spiritual wisdom.

Think about your relatives in terms of religious beliefs. How many religions are represented in your family tree?

Find out how your family has used religion in their lives.
Are they actively religious or merely members of a religion?
Are you aware of any prejudices towards other religious groups in your family?

Start with your Great Grandparents:
Inquire into their religious backgrounds.
Did they follow the religious mandates of their time? Did they live their lives in one place or were they transported to new places or cultures?
Did they suffer or struggle because of their religious beliefs?
Did they hate or fear any other religions?

Grandparents:
Grandparents carry the spiritual chi (energy) that is passed—skipping a generation—to their grandchildren. Whether or not you have ever known them, their gift to you is of a spiritual nature.

Inquire about their religions. Are there any stories you have heard about their lives that could relate to their religious belief systems or experiences?

What did your grandparents tell your parents about God?
What did your grandmother or grandfather tell you about God?
What did your parents tell you about your grandparents' religious beliefs or experiences?
What were the cultural aspects of their religious holidays, etc.?

Think about your Parents:
Are they from the same religion?
What did they tell you about God?

What are their religious prejudices?

Did they make you go to church?

Did they ask you if you wanted to be confirmed?

Do you remember any remarks they have made about other churches or religions?

Are they afraid of those from very different religions and cultures?

Are your parents, or you, Atheists or Agnostics? What would that mean to you?

Think about Your Own Spiritual Story:

Ask yourself about the source of your religious beliefs.

Who influenced you the most in terms of religion?

Who instilled fear of God in you?

Who taught you about sin and hell?

Were you taught that you would be punished for your sins?

Who taught you about salvation?

Are you still practicing the same religion you were brought up in?

Would you marry someone from another religion?

Have you ever felt ashamed or embarrassed about practicing your religion?

Have you changed religious allegiance in this life?

Do you secretly despise or fear any others whose religious faiths are different than your own?

Do you feel any direct connection to The Divine? Under what circumstances does that happen?

Do you feel the most connected in a religious place such a church, or in nature?

Do you think there is a difference between religion and spirituality?

Do you pray? Everyday—, or when you feel frightened?

Ask yourself about your own deepest religious thoughtforms. What are the religious concepts that influence you most?

Do you think that your relationship with God is affected by your gender?

Do you see God as a male, father god?

Do you think there is a personal god who is watching your life?

Do you pray for God to reward you for praying?

Do you think others are Divine, or only special religious people such as saints?

Do you think priests and ministers are closer to God than yourself?

Do you feel inspired by sermons?

Do you go to church for yourself or because others expect you to?

Do you attend religious services mostly on holidays, or regularly?

Do you stay focused in church, or do you fall asleep, or go over other pressing situations in your life during sermons?

Do you look forward to your day of worship?

Do you think God is listening and watching you?

Do you feel that God is punishing you through all the difficult aspects of your life?

Do you believe in reincarnation?

Do you think you chose this lifetime?

Do you feel that karma is retribution?

Do you think enlightenment will free you from the wheel of karma?

Did you want to be born?

Could you imagine yourself as a religious authority in this lifetime or any other?

I know that some of these questions will cause you to contemplate very deeply. Listen to the first thought that comes so that you will know what is actually true for you, whether or not you would divulge the answers to anyone else.

NOTES FOR TRACKING YOUR OWN SPIRITUAL REPERTOIRE

Great Grandparents

NOTES FOR TRACKING YOUR OWN SPIRITUAL REPERTOIRE

Great Grandparents

NOTES FOR TRACKING YOUR OWN SPIRITUAL REPERTOIRE

Grandparents

Notes for Tracking Your Own Spiritual Repertoire

Grandparents

NOTES FOR TRACKING YOUR OWN SPIRITUAL REPERTOIRE

Parents

Notes for Tracking Your Own Spiritual Repertoire

Parents

Notes for Tracking Your Own Spiritual Repertoire

Your Own Spiritual Story

Notes for Tracking Your Own Spiritual Repertoire

Your Own Spiritual Story

TWELVE

The Technology of Consciousness—Exercises

"THE TECHNOLOGY OF CONSCIOUSNESS—EXERCISES" **is the most important chapter of this book**. It offers a way through the frustrations we all feel about the god conversation and it shows us exactly how we can change through the format of Exercises in Consciousness. In our hearts we know that god wars on any level are not who we are. Our self-righteous religious beliefs bring us negative emotions and disharmony. "Never speak socially about politics or religion" they tell us, but we have come to a place where we not only must speak out, we must change how these things effect our lives.

Perhaps we feel a spiritual knowing, but cannot move past the mental arena to one of deep experience and we know that we are caught in the quagmire of our religious background, feeling helpless to break free. We may blanket ourselves in the comfort of our faith or beliefs, but all the while we sense an immovable block that separates us from a powerful energy we know is there somewhere. We want to reach it and at the same time we are terrified to even question whether it exists.

We all want to live in a more enlightened spiritual world, but we do not know how to make the changes necessary to do it. We have never found a way through our minds, emotions (or our religions) into a place of clarity and connection to our own spiritual truths, most of which reside just on the other side of our conscious awareness.

I created this "technology of consciousness" to help us truly release the blockages that keep us from being free of restrictive belief systems and the fears they engender in us. We will accomplish this partly through clearing memories stored in our bodies.

Memory is not only locked within the brain centers, but in actuality, every cell of the trillions of cells in our body has mind, and therefore memories. The mind of the cell is like an infinite computer that records untold experiences and nuances through our many sensory faculties. They are actually all stored as cellular memory.

There are infinite points within the matrix of our multidimensional bodies that are triggered through association and encoded reference, which engineer not only our genes but also the structure of our reality. We can access them consciously and energetically to free ourselves from those that hold us in repetitive karmic patterns.

You may think that you do not remember the first time you went to church or heard the word "God," but you do. You may think that your past is lost in a sealed container that can never be reopened, but it can easily be opened and it is orchestrating your choices right now.

Your body will help you open your memory banks and flush out their contents so that it can be free of a life ruled by association and repetition. First we will retrieve memories that will help to free you, and then we will clear them so that they can no longer be the silent manipulators of your life. It is these memories that repeat the past, magnetize the present and design the future.

The physical body is made of light, and therefore light is the best language of communication between our consciousness and the mind of the cell. When the DNA replicates itself, it uses ultraviolet light in a liquid medium. Each color of our visible spectrum is a frequency of light with its own specific speed and length. When you ask your body what color it needs to dissolve a memory, release a thoughtform or feeling, it will show you an exact tone or shade of the color it needs. It may show you one color and then another, two colors at once, or an entire rainbow. You may be shown opalescence, iridescence, or even perceive frequencies of light that don't actually exist in our "normal" reality.

You don't have to see the colors; you may hear the words or even feel them. If you hear or see black, ask again for a specific light, as black is not a color. It is an energy that lacks light and pulls light towards it. Often a place holding negative energies will appear black because there is no light or consciousness within it. We also do not utilize the frequency of grey because it amplifies a dying energy, depressive and heavy. If it is a silvery grey, it will provide a quickening galactic frequency, which is excellent. The body is a master in terms of light frequencies and you can trust it implicitly to show you exactly what it needs. The trick is to not try to choose for the body, but let it instruct you.

We will go through the first Exercise in Consciousness using one theme and then you can practice the pattern using any question that is relevant to you. It does not take long to do this, but you need to be somewhere alone so that you are not disturbed for a short time.

Before we access our religious memories, we will work for a moment in the body to warm up so that you can truly allow and trust your body to take you into experiences and memories. Read over the exercise several times or even tape it so that you know exactly what you are doing.

First, close your eyes and take some deep breathes in order to allow your consciousness to turn inward.
Then, ask your body to show you where you hold fear of God. (Even if you think you don't, you can be sure that you psycho-genetically carry within you such fear.)
You may feel a sensation somewhere in your body or inner organs, you may hear the place or see it in your mind's eye.

Bring your consciousness into that place and become aware of the fear. Let yourself touch it. Is it tight, dark, heavy?

Ask your body what color it needs to release this fear of God. Take the first color or colors that come to your mind and imagine you are sucking the color into the place in your body and that this beautiful light frequency is washing away the fear. Let the light absorb the fear until you feel a shift.

Now ask your body where it holds a sense of love or connection to the Divine Source.

Again, bring your consciousness into that place in your body and imagine opening the encapsulation of the energy so that it begins to flow into every cell of your body. Then, extend it out from you into the world. Imagine it entering into any situation, person, or place that needs this Divine connection.

Ask your Higher Self to show you a positive, spiritual attribute you hold.
It could be a sense of compassion, love, generosity, caring for nature, et cetera.
Ask your body where you hold that attribute.

Bring your conscious awareness into that place and imagine you could open it so that the spiritual energy flows through every cell of your body.

As you can see, these Exercises in Consciousness can use either a negative or positive focus to rebalance and clear religious imprints. Are you ready to practice these exercises and make changes in your life? Remember that rebalancing will bring you a sense of grace because they are not about confusion in the mind, but about a new kind of peace inside yourself that will open you to the evolution of God as a part of your own Soul's journey.

Here are some other themes that are important to explore:
Where do I hold fear of other religious sects or religions?

Remember that you may not be conscious of these fears or prejudices because you have inherited them from ancestors and they are below your conscious awareness. Do not resist them. Simply ask your body to show you where they are, and focus in that place.

Go through all religions that you can name and hold each one in your mind's eye. Ask your Higher Self (your intuitive inner voice) to show you a negative thoughtform that you have to be cleared about that religion, at this moment. E.g., Christians are the only righteous ones, Muslims are violent, Hindus are ritualistic, Jews are the "chosen ones," et cetera.

Your conclusions about other religions may be the result of cellular memories that harken back to cultures or places that have left residues in your psyche.

Ask your Higher Self to show you any place, or culture that you need to clear.

Ask that place or culture to take form in your mind's eye. You might perceive prayer rituals, a face, a landscape, et cetera.

Ask what color they need from you to be released. Draw that color in and radiate it out to them until they disappear.

You may be surprised at what comes into your consciousness. Your thoughtforms may be coming from psychogenetic imprints your family, culture, or religion have instilled deeply within your being. You may not even think you believe these perspectives. We all like to think that we are free of prejudices, but we are not. Nevertheless, they are inside us and can influence our life—and, in fact, our world!

Become conscious of your negative thoughts. You can actually hear yourself thinking them. Then, do this Exercise in Consciousness to clear not only the thoughtform, but to alter the pattern of consciousness.

Ask your body where it is holding that negative thoughtform.

Ask it what color it needs to release it.
Imagine that you are sucking that color into the place where the negative thoughtform is stuck and let the color dissolve it.

In the same manner, clear guilt, salvation, deserving, sin, and unworthiness. There are many words that describe religious themes you can release.

When I am working with people to release their religious themes and I ask them what are the thoughtforms they have about themselves and God, "unworthiness" and not being "good enough" are major themes.

Another theme to contemplate is that of pleasing God. Ask your Higher Self to illuminate your unconscious needs and conclusions about how to please God and then clear them all from your body.

The more esoteric themes such as reincarnation and fear of galactics are also important.

Ask your body to take you into any memory or experience in this lifetime where you felt fear of galactics (aliens, extraterrestrials). (A fearful scene in a movie or book may come to mind, or something someone was telling you, or even a direct experience of galactic energies surrounding you—abductee or contactee.)

Allow yourself to enter the scene and ask what was the thoughtform or conclusion that came to you, i.e., galactics would hurt you? Overpower you?

Ask your body where you are holding that thoughtform in your body.

Ask what color that place needs to release the thoughtform.

Draw that color into the area and wash out the thoughtform.

Ask your body where it is holding the entire episode with all its images and feelings.

Ask what color it needs to release the memory entirely so that it is not a point of reference or repetition.

An additional adjunct of this exercise, and all such themes where another being is part of the equation, is to release them so that you truly know you are not the victim or bound by anyone but yourself.

Ask that person (God, the devil, the galactic) what color they need from you to come into balance and harmony in your life now.

Draw that color down from the cosmos through the top of your head and send it out from your stomach (solar plexus) to them. Imagine a laser of that light entering into them until they disappear from your mind's eye.

Now, take a deep breath and draw white light from the cosmos in the same way down through the top of your head, filling your body and extending it out through your solar plexus.

This clears your consciousness so you can lift up into higher awareness and feel the lightness that comes from using the power of choice to create your life.

The concept for "The Evolution of God" came to me many years ago when we began to see that people who came to the Sanctuary of Light church for spiritual guidance were very conflicted about who they were in relationship to God. I designed a clearing process utilizing the multi-incarnational format we employ at The Light Institute so that they could consciously access the source of their spiritual dilemmas. Our unique technology of consciousness allows a person to perceive lifetimes related to spiritual issues. Themes of clearing God, angels, suffering, heretics, religions, death, mystics, ascension, transcendence, etc., are truly breathtaking when experienced from inside a scene expressing the hologram of those realities. (See Chapter 13, *God and Reincarnation.*)

THIRTEEN

GOD AND REINCARNATION

A LARGE PORTION OF THE EARTH'S POPULATION now considers reincarnation a plausible ingredient for the Soul's journey. Whether we abhor endings, or whether we simply resonate with the infinity of evolution, we are beginning to see that a single human lifetime is not even a flicker in the great cosmic pulse. We want more than one, and our expanding consciousness is showing us that this is an intelligent view. We know we have much to learn and we can glimpse a purpose of living in multiples as a format for growth on octaves beyond our own lives. It is simply not enough to be alive for a moment and then be snuffed out with no further options than the possible genetic echo into future generations.

If we entertain the spiral of evolution, we can see that a life may not only touch the future, but that it may actually connect the future to the past because of its own essence of seeding material, which creates a kind of magnetic energy groove that attracts relevant energies to it. We can actually alter the future by changing the remnants of the past that are crystallized in our psychogenetic patterns.

One of the obstacles to our enlightenment of the cosmos is our confusion of linearity and the constriction of time on a continuum. It is almost impossible for us to comprehend that "past lives" are going on now—that time pulses and is spatial, but is not simply a linear thread. Incarnations ripple out through the cause and effect laws of karma, which means that individual events or lifetimes are simply points of reference within the matrix of the third dimension that bleed in and out of unmanifest realities.

Subtle energetics from one lifetime can show up as an accumulative effect, like recessive genes, and alter the course of reality. Spiritually, this can be very positive as those traits that support intelligence, love or power, can greatly facilitate spontaneous juxtaposition from one point in the hologram of incarnations to another. The experiences, gifts of wisdom, belief systems and emotional compositions of those lifetimes are with us today. If we access their source by finding and releasing those lifetimes, we can filter or disperse them to our benefit. The spiritual opportunity is to extract the highest octave of potential and purpose from any situation and imprint it as an essential attribute.

In the same way that our childhood set the perimeters of who we think we are in the present, the imprints of the "past" relive themselves through repetition until we have mastered or become illuminated through those experiences—irrespective of the number of embodiments. They are repeated not because we are held to unfinished themes, or bound by punishment for past deeds, but because negative energies are very strong magnetically and attract again and again similar constructs: "like attracts like."

You can see those very laws in play in this present lifetime. Think how many times you have experienced rejection, disappointment or loss. The reoccurring themes bring certain conclusions that cause you to say to yourself, "See, this always happens." Your very expectations are the actual **cause** of your experiences, because you are attracting them through your limited scope of self-professed probabilities.

Most of the concepts about reincarnation are caught in the limiting web of negative one dimensional tallying good against bad and implied retribution for the "evil" of our ways. What we hold in our minds, or believe, is what we reinforce or bring into form. Thus, the mythology of the past is recreated in the present third dimension as reality. It is time to take reincarnation out of the simplistic terms of the past cultures and religious beliefs, and see it in the light of our present consciousness. We think of reincarnation through the view of the body, rather than that of the Soul. If we could see its value in terms of Soul evolution, we could advance our consciousness in catapultic leaps. Reincarnation and rebirth must be included in any serious conversation about God because we simply cannot perceive the scope of The Divine through the small peephole of one body, or master the cosmic laws of karma without a more amplified perspective.

Action and reaction are bound together by a cosmic thread that is not cut by death. Events of other lifetimes pursue us even into future incarnations of the Soul. Their markings are etched into our spiritual and emotional DNA as well as our physical DNA and find us in any environment or body we inhabit. It is not that we can or should attempt to escape them, but rather, they provide the windows into evolutionary mechanisms that can free us from the "treadmill" aspect of reincarnation.

I am not saying that if we learn all our lessons and become detached from mundane reality that we will get off the wheel of karma and no longer incarnate. That is a misconception that has been passed down from all corners of spiritual teachings. The hope of being released from the bonds of existence is like a view from the inside of a cubicle. We cannot see that the outside is interwoven with the inside.

The cosmos will always depend on matter to frame the unmanifest. We will always exist. The Buddha said, "All life is suffering." Compared to nirvana, to the void? Yet, we have our moments—in the beauty of nature, making love, giving birth, in the stillness of meditation, et cetera. We extend powerful energies into the cosmic sea. Through awakened consciousness we will be able to use the power of transfiguration from one level of cosmic existence to another with the grace of mastery. It is our true potential and we can begin now! Embodiment could be "heaven on earth." It will occur when human consciousness can hold awareness in multidimensional holograms.

Christian dogma resists reincarnation, because it is seen as contrary to heaven. The idea that heaven is eternal, yet "earned" in one lifetime is a bit far fetched. It is the usual enticement that if you are good, you will live forever in "the house of the Lord." Heaven has been imagined as a place we go as the selves we recognize now. If you are a male, will you reside forever in that body in heaven? If you are in body to learn, why would you experience from only half your genetic equation? If you are a woman, where is the lesson of the male? Why is it so difficult for us to let go of our bodies and perceive ourselves as Souls—without the crude division of male and female or the emotional personality of the present?

Our insistence of "place" is a rather limited human perspective of finding truth. If heaven and hell are places we go after our lives, from what place do we come? We know it is not heaven, though we may feel we have been sent from heaven because it is the only focal point of the cosmos with which we have some mythology. Where, then, in the conversation of place, is our source? In the future we will expand our frame of reference to include whole galaxies, and we will contemplate this question from a very different point of view.

We feel that we must decorate reality with some kind of recognizable and visible substance in order to feel secure, but our true orientation does not come from our body, or a place, it comes from the centering of our Soul. To find this, we must use consciousness to discover our true selves. If heaven were a place of serenity and love, it would be the perfect environment from which to prepare an incarnation. We could see clearly our past choices and their results, and set a blueprint for themes to master in a new incarnation.

I would offer that heaven is a state of consciousness; one that can be entered at any moment—not simply after death or before life. We are not accidents or freshly formed bodies with no former context. At the very least, we hold the perspectives of our forefathers as reference within our DNA, thus we are imbued with the ongoing pulse of life. The Soul has infinite incarnations as reference and certainly is not extinguished by the demise of an incarnate body.

We knew earth before we got here and there are other places we know as well. The cycles of memory and the progression from one reality to another are as innate to life as birth and death.

Rebirth is the recycling of energies in accordance with cosmic law. "Energy never dies, it just changes form." It renews itself by recomposing into ever more varied forms.

It is not strange to contemplate reincarnation. We all have feelings and knowings that come from some other arc of time that nevertheless belong to us. They come as vague flickers of recognition that include all our senses of sight, smell, touch, sound, and others—places, people and feelings are familiar without any rational supposition as to why they are.

Imagine for a moment that through your ancestors, your incarnations, and your infinite Soul you were there in the naked past when God was given a name on earth. The fear of the God Force would have been instilled collectively in your tribe and permeate all your actions in terms of setting the pattern of not displeasing "God."

Those primordial imprints are with you today, instilled in the past, seeded through you into the future of generations even beyond your present embodiment. Not only may you be the "carrier" of such imprints, but future generations themselves may have been in body during those epochs and through that commonality with you, be drawn into your life experience. This is a perfect example of the laws of karma, cause and effect, and why we perennially return to body carrying with us themes we have touched before.

Children seem to begin replaying reincarnational memories from about the age of four when they can create whole scenarios replete with multiple characters and environments. The themes they present are similar to adult themes: relationship, helping others, power, good guys, bad guys, and others. If one were to listen to these playacting vignettes from the perspective of reincarnation, one would have a glimpse into the spiritual repertoire of a Soul residing within the body of the child. Children are fully developed Souls!

I developed multi-incarnational techniques at The Light Institute of Galisteo as a format to uncover the true source of our longings, our fears and our own spiritual attributes, without the debris of our judgments and automated recordings of truth instilled by culture, religion and home. It has now been twenty-three years of incalculable information gathered from children, scientists, religious leaders, and every manner of person who has chosen to delve into cellular memory. What comes to them is their own, without suggestion or influence from us.

Our work allows profound clearing from the gamut of human emotions, bodily issues, and spiritual themes. In fact, the desire to write this book came from the astounding results of explorations into the "God theme." We facilitate lifetimes of spiritual themes that might include those in which a person died for God, feared God, spoke for God, carried godly energy in body, experienced transcendence, found their Divine Source, and infinite others that brought peace and illumination.

Exploring incarnations through their themes is a powerful way to learn about yourself and your spiritual evolution. You may have a theme about your relationship with the God Force that you have expressed through many time zones, cultures or bodies, and opposite points of view. In each one, you may have played different roles within the theme. You may have been the devout follower, the reformist, the atheist, et cetera.

Do you have an inkling of the Crusades? Do the images of knights, armor, swords cause a reaction in you? Do the smells of religious rites stimulate fragmental flickers in your brain? Does the frightening power of déjà vu whisper to you to pay attention when you find yourself in any religious scenario? You may be very deeply entrenched in your Catholic faith and feel fear of other religious advocates such as Muslims, Jews, or Seiks. Quite possibly these negative grooves are your own repertoire from other incarnations as well as anything you might have been taught in this lifetime.

You may have been the victim of blood letting from another religious group in the past and the unconscious fear is still with you. Just as likely, you may have been a religious aggressor slaughtering others in the name of your god. Those you have hurt by your thoughts or actions need to be rebalanced through your conscious awareness so that you can expand your own hologram of positive potential—and above all, free yourself, and them, from the vicious cycle of repetition.

Forgiveness is a word used often in relation to the victims and the victimizers. "Forgive those who trespass against you" takes on an entirely new meaning within the context of reincarnation. On the one hand it is easier to forgive if we recognize the possibility that someone who has hurt us may have been hurt by us in another lifetime. On the other hand, there is no need to use forgiveness as a self-righteous gesture when we comprehend that we have chosen everyone around us to teach us the lessons we have selected to learn. Within spiritual law, they are our closest Soul friends! This does not mean that causing pain is acceptable through karmic laws or that our suffering is our fault. It means that we are part of everything that happens to us and that we must seek its purpose in order to free ourselves from the bondage of being victims. We can only know that purpose through the spiritual illumination of multi-incarnations.

We can take responsibility from a spiritual octave much easier than struggling to defend our victimhood. There is a recognizable power in perceiving the hologram of action and reaction. If we see that our experiences at the hand of others are coming from a scenario beyond this lifetime, it brings us great solace and courage to balance or release what needs to be freed from the residues of our Soul's evolution. As we experience life from all points of the hologram, we evolve because we have the gamut of reference from the victim to the victimizer and all the players in-between.

Do not be afraid to discover that you have played the "bad guy," the victimizer. Everybody carries a sense of guilt or fear of being bad within them, because we all have the imprints of other lifetimes within our cellular memory. It is a great relief to know all your points of reference and many people actually enjoy expressing these negative energies from the perspective of another lifetime, once removed from their present body. It is wonderful to actually see oneself in those scenarios and then disengage from them through the technologies of consciousness. Until they are flushed from the depository of the cell, they will stay with you throughout whole series of incarnations—poisoning your reality and bringing pain and suffering to you and those you love for generations to come. You can prevent this! (See Chapter 12, *Technology of Consciousness*.)

What happens to purgatory and hell within the potential of reincarnation? Does the spirit burn in hell for some designated allotment of suffering and then reincarnate again? In effect, this is the law of karma that opens the way through all impossible, hopeless and painful realities to continue the inevitable evolution of the Soul! No, we do not "burn in hell" forever. The dastardly deeds of one lifetime cannot stop the pulse of infinity and are eventually rebalanced by their opposites of compassion and goodness in other incarnations. Why do we fear the possibility of reincarnation? The entire gamut of extremes resides within us because of our many lifetimes, and awaits only our choice—who do we want to be?

Intrinsic to this conversation of rebirth are the fantastic possibilities it provides from a spiritual perspective. If through some trigger of consciousness you could relive other incarnations specifically through a spiritual focal point, you would find ones in which you had ecstatic experiences of cosmic bliss, experiences of absolute peace and serenity. What would happen if you saw through the veil into the astral sleeve of lifetimes and focused your themes on God and spirituality? I am sure that you would begin to see beyond the content of those incarnations into levels of profound essence in which you could find new meaning for life. Each life illumination would help you to remember the oneness that you seek deep within your being.

Each time you incarnate, you may select a different body, culture and religion. If you could hold them in your consciousness, truth would appear differently from each point of view. The hatred, the fear and the righteous battles in God's name would disappear. In fact, most of what you think is true would change. It would become clear to you that these lives are all reverberating through your reality at this very moment and creating the uniqueness of your being. Each attribute could be traced back to a kind of source wherein you garnered the wisdom to master a theme. There are almost infinite qualities that you have used in your multi-incarnations that you can activate in this lifetime.

Imagine that those Souls who were present at the time of any of our great spiritual advancements have returned again to body. What would be the mandate of those Souls in this incarnation? Would they see the limits of their former consciousness? Would they experience their teachers from a present perspective of spiritual awareness or from that of another religion? Would they even choose religion? The most fascinating question is: "Are we they?" If we have many lifetimes, our relationship with the Divine Source can be different each time, affording us wonderful opportunities to embrace our own divinity through so many bodies and environments.

Each illumination that comes to our consciousness gives us access to even greater possibilities, not only in terms of knowing God, but also who we are and what we can become. The information that awaits human consciousness through accessing reincarnational repertoire is almost inexhaustible. "Incarnations of the Soul" are not limited to human form, nor do they always occur here on this planet.

Many people ask why if they have had beautiful, spiritual lifetimes, they feel so unenlightened now. They wonder how they could have had spiritual knowledge on a high level and now find themselves struggling in the mundane realities of their present existence. Spiritual mastery is not a linear or consecutive path. A great spiritual master could return to embodiment as a drunkard or novice in order to thread an important spiritual theme that had not been incorporated before. Perhaps that being understood cosmic law, but had no connection to love or compassion, necessitating an incarnation on another level of life's hologram. Sometimes it seems that we are regressing, but we are merely taking up the threads whose composite strength is necessary to weave the matrix of enlightenment.

The concept of reincarnation has ramifications far beyond the possibility of repeated embodiment as a means of evolution, it opens our consciousness to new realities that we could not otherwise glimpse. If we move to the awareness of universal energetics we can perceive cycles of rebirth in new contexts. Does God, the Divine Source, reincarnate or transfigure as a part of evolution—or do we just hold to the myths of the past when people were influenced by visions? We are beyond the pulse of holding onto God; we must open to the incoming energies.

In the time of the Goddess, we saw that energy as feminine. After the priests took over, the God Force became a masculine image. There, God and all his emissaries stayed—from Buddha, to Christ, to Muhammed. Are these reincarnations of God, or are they the dressings of man? Are there Buddha and Christ revisions of each other the way we are all one Soul, or have we entrapped our god or gods in the astral so that we cannot allow their evolution? What would that look like now? It seems logical that any "second coming" of a god figure would never be a repetition of the old. We have been waiting for something that is already transcended.

We must realize that we are still holding all of our godly templates in the very clothes they wore, the cultures they were born into, and their teachings in the encapsulation of the time reference in which they appeared. We have not explored their embodiment within all time and places. We have not learned to revisit them within their essence. We have described them as godly by their manifestations, not their essence. It is not the glowing lights, the radiant white rods, the fire, the clouds (which may suggest galactic tools of power) that make one God. How interesting that the yang universe equates God only with power, control and even covenant! These are the signposts of unenlightened man relating to more advanced beings—who may have nothing to do with being God.

It is not the power shown over matter or life that makes one God—it is the presence of Divine Source, the ultimate genesis of the self and the cosmos. That is God—and it is not bound by culture or galaxy, but by our recognition of it—by essence—our very own!

We will forever come forth from the unmanifest into the manifest worlds so that what we gather through physical focus can be offered back to further the evolution of the Divine Source. Once we have cleared the concept that embodiment is separation from God, and therefore some kind of punishment, we will embrace the sacred opportunity of embodiment as the fantastic adventure it is.

Perhaps the greatest gift of reincarnation is its potential to free us from the bondage of primordial survival instinct that prevents us from expanding our horizons beyond the plea to be saved from death. The experience of many births and deaths is the key to overcoming the fear of death, the end of existence. When we truly know that consciousness is not entrapped in body, that we will always survive, then we will reach out with the curiosity and sense of exploration necessary to open new worlds.

EVOLUTION

1. Release any conclusion that you cannot believe in heaven and reincarnation.

2. Clear any fear you have of reincarnation. (See Chapter12, *Technologies of Consciousness.*)

3. Imagine that you are in an incarnation in which you are the template of God. Feel the Divine goodness radiating from you out into the world.

4. Imagine that those you have envisioned as godly could appear in a new form and context. How would you experience them?

FOURTEEN

GODS AND GALACTICS II*

"GODS AND GALACTICS" IS A DISCUSSION we can only have if you are willing to explore the possibility that we are not alone in the great cosmos of universes. Can you imagine the repercussions of such a new truth? When we are finally able to break through the barriers of time and space, we will indubitably find ourselves in the midst of other cosmic species who will blast away the last shreds of our "truths" about everything from science, to technology, to God.

Today, scientists are speculating that there must be other sentient lifeforms beside ourselves in this tiny speck of the galaxy. They are seeking in earnest and what they discover will change human destiny forever. Tomorrow, we will confirm that there are civilizations more advanced than ourselves, and those less than ourselves, spread out across the seas of stars.

That awareness has a more profound significance than just the theme of supremacy or expedient advancement in terms of relating to other cosmic beings. If we look at it from the perspective of our vision of God, we can see that it has the potential to entirely undo or alter all the religious tenants we uphold. Nevertheless, we must look at the possibilities it could bring to us. If we realize that we are truly part of the vast cosmos, we might begin to experience a sense of spiritual oneness that will take us beyond the constrictions of form.

Our concept of God must evolve to embrace the knowledge of the infinite Divine Source beyond human form and reference. Consciousness is not entrapped in our human DNA. It needs no breath, no arms, legs or ears. It can move between old and new bodies, be shared or superimposed onto something else, instilled into any kind of matter while it permeates the entire cosmos. If we can begin to think of "God" in terms of pure consciousness instead of as the template of our own form, we will be ready to discover possibilities that have not come to our awareness in the past.

Earth is just one of zillions of planets orbiting untold suns. Astronomers have already found an earth-like planet orbiting a red star in a neighboring solar system! It is not unlikely that more advanced civilizations across the universes have perfected and coalesced their consciousness into bodies similar or vastly different than ours. Are they gods? Only from our limited, comparative perspective. We have not reached the horizon of consciousness as of yet, so we search our galactic skies for possible duplicates of ourselves— earth, water, air and the carbon matrix. As we come to understand that life may exist in radically different forms, not based on the same prerequisites as life on earth, we will open to the brilliant awareness that the others are also free of such limitations.

As our knowledge expands, we may find that what we concluded was the "one and only God" is no more than a galactic "Lord" with the minuscule domain of our solar quadrant. By opening to this awareness, we may begin to see the core of our relationship and definition of God through entirely new perspectives.

Perhaps we have clutched at the human kind of God because to do otherwise would deeply confuse our sense of who we are. It is possible that advanced beings we have called gods, simply used our genetic image to create an interface that would be comprehensible to us in our human environment and level of consciousness.

As we begin looking into our own solar system for clues as to the mysteries of life, we will discover that cosmic laws include far more possibilities for living beings than we had imagined. Our children's children will travel out beyond our solar system and will not only marvel at the infinity of the Divine Source, but also about how we could not see what for them will be so obvious—our perception of God was too small! They will not believe in God the way we and our forefathers have, because they will encounter many diverse lifeforms of great power and accomplishment that we would have encased in the term—God.

They will come upon the points of origin whereby species were created through genetic manipulation and harvested or modified to fit the needs of the galactic scientists who created them, and the areas of the cosmos to which they were sent to begin life. This is not in contradiction to the theme of "God, the Creator." The genetic experiments that have gone on for eons within the galaxies are based on refocusing genetic patterns to create various species out of already existing DNA. We do not yet know how to create the original spark.

This acknowledgement may help us to comprehend the origins of our collective mythology that the gods created humans several times without success before they accepted our species. It was not about imperfection, evil, or displeasing God. It was not about original sin! In fact, the key to the myth is a reference to the gods themselves. They had great powers according to the myths, but they were inexact at the art of creating a species that would serve their purposes—whatever those were. In truth, they were not gods, but rather cosmic scientists attempting to create Homo sapiens to fit the environment of earth within certain contexts of their own design.

What was their purpose? Were they trying to make a species that would become their own experimental research? Perhaps they were attempting to create lifeforms that would do their bidding, as some people suggest. Most importantly, who are we to them; do they see us as raw material or low level unconscious beings that they can manipulate? Were they posing as gods because that is the only reference we have for superior intelligence?

Think how easy it is be become what others think you are. How convenient to wield the title of god over those who have no comprehension of what is really happening. Did they instigate the concept of a jealous god to protect their control over humans? You may find this difficult to accept at first, but if you will imagine the possibilities of space, it will become more plausible to you.

In thousands of reincarnational sessions, we have heard the recall of people immersed in this scenario of genetic manipulation. What is illuminating to me is that so many of them describe identical scenes: a genetic laboratory larger than planet earth with honeycomb style cubicles in which genetic formulas are grown. They tell of source material gathered from many galaxies and experimented with to create new life forms. It is speculated that this tactic was carried out here on earth during the time of Atlantis. The centaur, and many other strange creatures were the result of such experiments. Were these activities carried out under galactic tutelage or command? We can only guess. I think that most, if not all the Greek gods are of such origins.

The blue Vishnu deity of Eastern origin is a god form that has always fascinated me. According to the Hindu Bhagavad Gita, Vishnu has a cosmic form that encompasses energies beyond human perception. In his visible state, he is purported to have four arms and is of a bluish color. Since one of the most powerful galactic forms that appears to people around the world is a beautiful blue light, I ponder the possibility of transfiguration. Is Vishnu a representative of this kind of galactic group?

Our scientists have advanced enough to take original components of life and organize them into clones or grow them, but we have not been able to initiate life. For the moment, that ability remains as a primary prerequisite to be called a god—the power to initiate life. That does not mean that advanced galactic beings have not found the key to this Divine power: We do not know.

After all these millennia we still do not understand the potential of creation. What is imbued into physical form that corresponds to perception, emotion, or the matrix of specific reality? The terrifying stories we have heard about abductees cause us to conclude that some species of galactics may have no innate emotional bodies or feeling structures that would allow compassion, or caring for others. We could have been created by galactics who instilled their own psychogenetics of power struggle and war within our matrix—i.e., our galactic gene pool. Yet, we could also imagine that very advanced civilizations eons ahead of us, may have refined raw emotion into a more impersonal yet unconditional kind of loving energy.

If only for the fact that we originate from a galaxy with the shared essential essence of carbon, we then hold galactic DNA. It may be easier to feel a connection to the galactic if you remember that all the planets are carbon based atoms and so are you. Earth is a body in a solar system, within a galaxy, within a universe—therefore, we are all galactic beings by definition. It is time for us to remove the stigma of sci-fi from the galactic conversation, because our future includes galactic connections—without a doubt. The question is not if we are of galactic origin, but how we can harvest the potential it offers us if we become aware of it?

We have angelic, devic, galactic DNA, as well as our human genetic genome. It is important to realize that we go through cycles of varied characteristics throughout our lives in the same way that we go through different stages as we grow up. The angelic DNA is anchored within the highest astral dimensions. Angels are a cousin species to humans. We see the angelic features and energetics in babies and small children.

The devic genetic encoding has to do with the astral dimension of the natural world and all the sentient beings within the mineral and vegetable kingdoms. Children see nature spirits and speak to them as if they existed in the third dimension. It is a pivotal point in their development when they discover that others do not see what they see and want them to cut themselves off from those realities and enter the limitations of our visual world.

Sometimes children perceive the presence of galactic entities and are afraid of them. Galactic frequencies are much faster than our own. We have happy folk tales about fairies and other creatures of the astral dimension, but almost all our galactic references are about dangerous aliens. Children are afraid of what their parents are afraid of, even if the adults have not mentioned it.

Galactic genetics are cosmic in source, yet often come into play when a person reaches the level that the mind links up with mechanical realities such as computers, etc., because they allow the holographic brain patterns that are germane to galactic frequencies.

I think it is safe to say that there were, and are still, a number of different galactics that have visited earth at various times and with different agendas. The negative demands of the lord of Abraham certainly conjure the possibility of an un-evolved, dispassionate galactic who seemed to have mastered scare tactics for the purpose of absolute control, rather more than enlightened grace. "Gods and Galactics" is a conversation about beings and other worlds of power that have interfaced with our own.

Are the stories of Sodom and Gomorrah testimony of nuclear battles or demonstrations of weapons of destruction played out on earth? Very possibly. Were those battles directed at humans because of their inherent "wickedness," or were they actually wars about control over Earth between different galactic groups? In the end, why do we want to continue with any god force that decimates and kills, or creates destruction?

May we ever be forewarned of the projection of gods onto ones who have strange powers. The most ancient imprint of God was, and still is, the fearful omnipotent ruler of the heavens who can destroy us at any moment.

The Mayan history is a good example of this, although it is echoed in the histories of many ancient civilizations. Their great knowledge of mathematics, astronomy, arts and sciences, as well as mastery over matter, remains a mystery to us. According to their own historical data, they had been visited by powerful gods who gave them tools for living—from new food crops, to healing, to organizing society, a calendar more correct than what we use today—and then left, saying that they would return. When they did not return, the Mayans, and others such as the Incas, fell to making sacrifices and offerings to bring the gods back to them. The blood baths were interminable and still the gods did not return.

The concept of sacrifice may have been instigated by galactic overlords whose mandate was to take life for purposes of their own. Were they playing with us to obtain genetic seed? The sacrifices we made had a negative effect on our genetic pool because we sacrificed the "best."

The story of the Mayan nobles playing a ball game in which the winners were sacrificed to the gods is a vivid example. How long would it take to wipe out the most successful, intelligent human strains? —Apparently, not long. Who were those gods who demanded the hearts of the pure and the brave? —Not the kind we want! They took hearts for genetic resource material without so much as a "permission granted" clause, thereby thrusting the principles of human conduct into the pit of darkness.

The law of permission is central to the evolution of humanity as it holds us to seek respect and equality in all our relationships. It is a psychogenetic imprint from the angelic realm. We "ask" permission through awareness of others whenever we enter their space—be it physical, emotional, or psychic in nature. In contrast, too many galactic encounters have occurred without that fragile balance of mutual agreement.

In reflecting on the caliber of galactics with whom we have interacted, it seems apparent that galactic prowess may have nothing to do with spiritual evolvement. This point has been a deep inner struggle for me, because I initially saw galactics through the lens of mechanical, non-feeling technological entities. I felt that they were the antithesis of anything spiritual in nature. Now I see that it is absurd to clump galactics into one grouping, because they are as different in mental and spiritual perspectives as we are in language groups—perhaps multiplied by trillions. Some galactics have reached levels of existence whereby unconditional love and oneness are the standards of life. There is a collective kind of consciousness that is not oneness by consensus, but an actual fusion of beingness.

Could there be a code of ethics for all galactic beings? We can be certain that their own laws of conduct are vastly dissimilar than our own by virtue of their cosmic realities. It is likely that concepts of good and evil, which may not exist for all of them, are entirely different than ours. Galactics may not have the same perspective on personal sin, and therefore salvation would not enter their conversation between humans and gods unless they were employing that same pattern of manipulation religions have perpetrated on their constituents since the very beginning of interpreting God. Both employed "placate God—or else" tactics.

From the perspective of a galactic portrayal as God, we can see how convenient it was to insure that humans were taught to allow only one god. Loyalty was the pact that sealed the relationship so humans would not "forsake" that god when another appeared, or in effect, allow any new information or experiences to intervene.

The Mayans described their gods as beings that outshone the sun in dazzling bodies of light. When the Spaniards arrived in their shinning metal armor, the Mayans thought the gods had come again and immediately acquiesced to their demands—initiating the absolute downfall and destruction of their civilization.

Psychogenetic imprints have been laid down within us all as to how we imagine God. As far back as thousands of years into antiquity we have texts that speak of "gods" in human or corporeal form coming and going from the sky in various kinds of space ships.

The most fascinating aspect about all the galactic god stories is the commonality of their references to flying machines. The Sanskrit Vaimanika Sastra drawings from India, dated around fourth century B.C.E., show several types of ships, including detailed descriptions of solar energy panels. How could this be? These drawings were done in a time of supposed simplicity without knowledge of any kind of machinery or non-organic energy source. Esoteric Tibetan books spoke of "pearls in the sky" referring to ships that appeared, while ancient Indian texts spoke of ships with fiery tails as well as the Bible's description of "chariots of fire."

Many early texts, including the Bible, are replete with vivid descriptions of the flying ships of the gods who were said to have arrived and departed in explosions of fire that describe quite accurately the liftoff of modern rockets. Here is a biblical example: Ezekiel 1:4 "I looked and I saw a windstorm coming out of the north—an immense cloud with flashing lightning and surrounded by brilliant light. The center of the fire looked like glowing metal."

The Dogon tribe of Africa drew explicit rocket designs in caves over four thousand years ago. They also drew exact trajectories of Sirius A, B and C. Sirius C was not calculated or even known to astronomers until 1995. Their mythology speaks of the gods arriving on earth in rockets coming from Mars where they stopped to prepare for landing on earth. They also say that the gods left because of the low level of consciousness of humans and promised to return when we evolved to a sufficient level as to be capable of truly communicating with them.

It does not seem too impossible in light of space travel today to entertain the idea that we have been visited by "gods" from other universes with whom interaction actually produced or altered human evolution. In fact, each time a great spiritual being has been present on Earth, we have seen a gigantic wave of change that has caused repercussions in the human psyche as well as profound advancement of knowledge.

Everywhere there are mentions of the gods seeding "the daughters of men." Did they take on human form in order to accomplish this? Think of Greek mythology in which the gods constantly veiled themselves in human bodies to influence or meddle in the affairs of men. What would have been the result of such crosses? Would these hybrids have had special abilities? We can only imagine. Are some of the clairvoyant abilities and spiritual predilections we have now the result of such galactic DNA?

Often the references speak of some of these gods as giants and then imply that their offspring were also large in physical size. The Bible says in Genesis 6:4, "There were giants in the earth in those days; and also after that, when the sons of God came in unto the daughters of men, and they bare children to them, the same became mighty men which were of old, men of renown."

When we consider the tales of giants on the land spoken of in the Bible and other recorded history and then view the mega-lithic idols of Easter Island, complete with astronomical data, we must ask ourselves if there isn't a correlation? The Olmecs of Mexico, thousands of miles away, had similar idols carved in unmovable stone. Yet there could have been no contact between them because the Easter Island megaliths seem to be from about 400 C.E. and the Olmecs were from1200 B.C.E. to about 400 B.C.E. The sacred statues of Tiahuanaco, the capital of pre-Incan civilization, are dated from thousands of years B.C.E., and yet exhibit the same giant stone beings.

Icelandic and Nordic ancient legends not only spoke of giants, but also actually used different names for the earth, sun or moon depending on whether the point of view was from men, gods, or giants! How could they have known those modern perspectives? The ancient Norsemen described the earth as a ball or sphere. Did they see it from above?

Perhaps the most misinterpreted galactics are the winged ones that are spoken of in many religions as angels. While our cousin angels are connected to the "Lord" of our heaven, not all winged beings are angels. Some galactics with large rather grey wings are completely different than the gentle angels of our astral dimension. What would we do with our angels, our priests, and our friends of God if we cast a futuristic, galactic eye onto religious dogma? No one wants to give up angels and the purity they represent. Most of all, no one wants to lose the comfort of protection, the hope of compassion, or the template of goodness they have provided throughout time. We have not stepped through the "windows to the sky" as yet, and thus we are unable to even decipher the difference between the angelic astral dimension most people believe in and the cosmic winged beings that have been spoken of as inhabitants of space.

Who are these angels/galactics who pass messages from "God?" From what level of lord do they speak? How can we know where to put our faith? It must always be our intuitive knowing that allows us to feel truth within the energetic qualities of higher beings who we can trust. One of the great teachings from my own Higher Self is that we are not afraid of the unknown. We are afraid of what stirs deeply within us as an amorphous memory. Galactic energies that touch our lives are, and will always be, somehow related to us. We can access those points of reference to discard those that do not support our evolution and bring forward those that do.

What we can trust is that we are on the brink of discoveries that will sever forever the concepts we have had about the God Force, and that we will have the most profound opportunity to free ourselves from the constrictions that held us back from experiencing divinity as an essence we share with all life, whatever its form or origin.

* "Gods and Galactics" appears as a chapter in my book, *Soul Bodies.*

EVOLUTION

1. Imagine God as a galactic energy that can open your consciousness to cosmic possibility.

2. Clear fear of galactic energies. (See Chapter 12, *Technology of Consciousness.*)

3. Clear any imprints you have about galactic beings, i.e., aliens.

4. Embrace the possibility that you are a galactic being with cosmic energies you can harvest now.

FIFTEEN

WHO IS GOD?
A NEW SENSE OF
THE DIVINE SOURCE

THE SEARCH FOR "G" HAS BEEN HUMANITY'S great quest since time immemorial. From the most silent supplication to the violence of the God wars, we have imagined, extrapolated, defended and died for whoever or whatever we have deemed our own private God. Yet, we are still as fanatical or unsure as ever about: "Who is God?"

It is doubtful that we will ever have a remotely definitive answer to this burning question until we can expand our search into a multidimensional hologram beyond our own reality. Whoever or whatever we call God exists beyond our world and we must reach out to those unknown realms if we are ever to truly know the Divine Source. We must learn to recognize the essence energies that make up the points of reference to the whole, within the context of universal creation. The Divine Source is pure light, infinite consciousness and the ever evolving, yet constant of all manifest and unmanifest dimensions.

Thus far, we have only been able to perceive a crystallized version of "who" is God. The incomprehensive Divine Source of the cosmos is light years beyond such a personified coalescence.

Who—is a compensatory title and description that helps us relate to it in human terms, but it cannot encompass that which is beyond periphery. The ultimate God has never been a simple one dimensional being who gave us commandments, ultimatums, or blessings—except in the narrow passageways of our primitive, linear minds. The possibility of cosmic, quadrant overlords or genetic creators may ultimately alter our sense of who we are and what we belong to as we reach deeper into the enfolding seams of the universes.

Our reality is third dimensional flesh and blood, and therefore it is understandable we would want and perceive a god that comes to our world in the way that we exist. But it is not to be. We have envisioned a "he" god with all of our own projections of fearful imagination, and thus we have bound ourselves to a vicious cycle of prophecy and prediction in which we see our doom as the abyss between ourselves and the comforting heaven we seek. The future holds incomprehensible realities for us and it behooves us to stretch out to meet it, rather than refuse to imagine "The Evolution of God." Beyond time and the laws of life we comprehend, there exists a creative flow that is expressed in incalculable forms, sculpted by a multi-faceted, conscious energy. We have seen barely one facet of its formless form. We belong to this Divine Source; and all that is—we belong to as well.

God is the ultimate template, not just for how to be good human beings, but how to be the essence of all beings. We could not live without some model of inspiration, some place to reach, some ideal to embrace; it is a human characteristic to seek, to wish to become what we see around us—in the same way that the child wishes to become as powerful, as loving, as knowing as its teacher or parent.

What if it were that when we prayed, we were indeed praying to the God within us, to the godly essence of which we are a part, so that we magnified and caused that for which we prayed—rather than an outside, unconnected power answering our prayers? We cannot seem to stretch our consciousness or expand it to include this holographic truth that all creation carries the energies of its creator, i.e., we pray to a God that is inextricably within us. This is why, since the beginning of existence, we have seen duality, manifested polarity, and lived in a world where we conclude that truth is either this or that, but cannot seem to be both.

Ancient Chinese philosophy teaches that "everything is connected to everything." Whatever we perceive as God, at some point at its farthest distance from us is simultaneously, intimately connected to our deepest, deepest essence. If we explore that, we will find God is indeed inside us; the Divine essence holds its power and its truth from within us. Perhaps this is the reason it is so important to let go of the aspects of the old god or gods that we have had and their commandments of limitation. We are ready for new guidance and new truths, truth and guidance that have to do with participating, not simply being acted upon by the cosmos.

Humanization of God has some glaring incongruities when placed within the context of the whole of the cosmos. We are not evolved enough to transfigure our bodies so that we can experience the universe and all its infinite life forms firsthand. We have had examples of this throughout time and from many different masters, yet we have not tried it ourselves—even though we have been encouraged to do so.

Many religious texts talk about how humans were made in the image of God. Is that because human form was our only repertoire in ancient times? Is it still? Could we even imagine godly form beyond our own genetic matrix? Use the name you wish and clothe The Divine in any form, but it will always remain above confines of description. We have used many allegories to express our relationship with God but they leave us in a state of longing, seemingly without recourse.

It is unfortunate to cut ourselves off from the communion with the Divine Source, because we only recognize it when we are convinced that it speaks exclusively through the human voice in commandments and words, and we can imagine it only through human personification. Those words, and written testaments of conversations with God seem authenticated simply because they exist. The ancient texts are addressed to those within the eras of their delivery, and much of their context is detrimental to the awakening of our consciousness now. We must open ourselves to new channels of relationship with God.

What about people today who feel they are having conversations with God? Why are they not heard or believed? I wonder—to what god are they speaking: the lord of our earthly domain, our solar system, our universe? Are they tapped into a recording of time and space? Do they know who it is that whispers to them? Whoever it is, is using their own human, cultural filter to reference truth as they can relate to it—not a code of truth that is beyond their belief capacities. However, we should listen to these messengers to garner any points of spiritual wisdom that could guide our evolution. If they are naysayers, they are not for us.

It is rather like the enigma of whether lightening simply strikes the earth or whether the earth magnetizes it. There is a synergy that links them together. Do such Divine conversations occur as if two people were talking, or is it that something causes an alteration in the internal state of consciousness of a person and they begin hearing their own godly essence (their Higher Self) coming to the fore of their awareness? Since this information or teaching is beyond the realms of their normal thought, they conclude it is an external force. If we practice holographic thought we begin to perceive that the inside and the outside are inextricable.

The problem for us is that we think of consciousness as something that belongs to a personality, a focused kind of intelligence, when in fact, the conscious creative energy of the cosmos is completely beyond such crystallization. The point in the center is no different than the infinite points that enclose the holographic, multidimensional periphery of God consciousness.

Why is this so frightening to us? Of course we are part of dimensions beyond the material plains, and that means that there is much buried beneath the external realities of our human existence. Surely we do not still elude ourselves that the Divine Source of all the infinite cosmos chooses human form as the highest octave. Unfortunately we do, because we have not met other sentient beings that can be our template. They exist and we are on the verge of encountering them. I wonder if we will allow them, embrace them or even recognize them?

Historically, we have seen the power of nature and called it God. We have felt the life giving energy of the sun and called it RA—the sun god. We have witnessed the moon pulling the tides into its magnetic embrace and we have called it God. We have worshiped elephants and plumed serpents. Why do we see God as nature? When asked about a moment in which we feel Divine presence, we often remember a moment in nature. Do we intrinsically know that The Divine sources nature, or is it that nature itself holds so much magical power and peace that it alters our perception, so we are embraced by a sacredness we describe as godly?

Over the millennia, some indigenous peoples developed the spiritual concept of the great circle of life in which everything is connected. The First Americans saw themselves as a part of nature, governed over by "The Great Spirit" that connected all beings. They recognized "the spirit in all things" whether it was a rock, a tree, or an animal. Each had its particular gift to give and that gift was held sacred—not feared.

When they killed an animal for food, the spirit of the animal was honored and felt to enter them. No part of the animal was discarded, as bone and tendon, flesh and skin were the gifts given them by their animal brothers. They celebrated life through ceremonies that expressed this connection. Before and after they hunted they dressed in the skins of their prey, and told their stories to honor them. They were more aligned to the ancient feminine teachings than the personification of a fearful and stern, masculine God.

Jesus, Muhammad, Moses, Buddha, etc., were men who brought wisdom to the world. The fight over whether they were Divine is not the point. Whether Jesus was the one and only Son of God is not the point. It is as if we are saying we must defend the divinity of Jesus so we can believe in him. Why don't we integrate his teachings so that we can become like him? Isn't it more inspiring to know him as a "godly man," a man by definition, a Divine being by essence? The godly human and the Divine being are one and the same—for Jesus and for us all! It is time to practice the spiritual teachings Jesus the Christ and the others bestowed on to humanity.

Did you know that Jesus was actually "voted" as Divine, the Son of God, by the Council of Nicaea, called together by the Roman emperor, Constantine, in 325 C.E.? Constantine converted to Christianity only in the end of his life when he saw that Christians were becoming a strong political power. Three hundred years after Jesus' death, the power of his presence ignited the fires of war between religious sects to establish his divinity, and therefore alter the political arena of the times. Belonging to one religion or another was a matter of life, war or even death, depending upon if you were on the prevailing side.

We don't fight over or insist on the divinity of Muhammad, Moses or Buddha. Buddha is a godly template because he became enlightened. He found a way to pass out of the pain of life into nirvana—or grace. Yet Buddha was a man, like Christ, like Muhammad, like other men who are not known to us but who carried and exemplified that Divine spark. There were women too, Isis, Quan Yin, Mary Magdalene, who performed miracles and brought universal knowledge. This should tell us something about our limited gender affiliation with God!

What would it have been like if we had decided that the God Force were feminine and kept the beliefs of the Goddess? Since only women can give birth, that would have been a natural conclusion because of the power of creation, yet ultimately we allowed words to rule over acts of creation.

Each of our Divine templates passed through initiations that opened them into greatness, into cosmic consciousness. All of them experienced the trials and tribulations of their connection to other realities and its effect upon daily existence. Their experiences offer us the great teaching that it is the "grace" with which we live our lives that anchors us into Divine essence. Everywhere in our lives exists the spiritual initiations that offer us illumination and greatness. They are often concealed in everyday experiences and we do not recognize them as such, so they slip by like the proverbial turning of the wheel of karma, and we miss our evolutionary opportunity because we do not see the connection.

If we could see past our emotions, our beliefs, our fears, we would realize that every dilemma has its purpose as an experience of consciousness. At The Light Institute we say, "What is the gift?" It is not that if we strive for a spiritual life we will be free of confusion or fear, it is that we will learn to trust our intuitive knowing and overcome the poison of emotional mind. The Divine Source lives within each and all humans, and every one of us has the choice to use that Source to evolve our lives and our world.

I wonder why it is that we feel so conflicted about whether there is one god or multiple representations of the Divine Source? Perhaps it is our fear that we would not be significant to more than one, or is it that the commandment of loyalty is so deeply ingrained in us psychogenetically? Why do we insist that honoring more than one god is tantamount to sinful unfaithfulness? The jealous god story seems more related to human conclusion than a dictate from an all-inclusive Divine Source.

Monotheism has contributed to the pretext for war amongst religious sects back into early Egyptian times. Even among the three major religions, hatred is instigated because of differences that are not so relevant as the pure God consciousness—in any way that it is perceived. For example, the Muslims decry Catholicism's belief in the Holy Trinity. Our universal spiritual connection is what should bring us together, not the form or belief systems in which we dress it. In this world of nuclear potential, we cannot continue on such perilous paths to mutual destruction because we are quibbling over godheads.

We have called each other "infidels" for too long and it must stop! What an odious word is infidel—the accusation of being unfaithful to God simply because one holds The Divine by different dogma.

Not only do we hold that there could only be one god, but we fight over who has the most favor with "him." Each of the major trinity, Jews, Christians and Muslims, has had their moment as "the Chosen" and then declared that that is the end of successions. It is not plausible or even possible to imprison the future of God only because we wish, or have been told, that there will be no change or evolution.

Many religions worship various gods, but what level gods are they? The "minor" gods, such as those revered for their specific areas of omnipotence, simply give us a point of reference for the various aspects or themes that are intrinsic to our lives. The problem with this is that we never see the possibilities of these attributes inside us—and therefore, do not embrace our Divine potential ourselves. We have so many fears about God. We fear that we will be punished or abandoned or that we are unworthy to face Divinity. If we can experience The Divine "within" us, all of those fears will vanish.

If we are part of the creative force—part of God through the virtue of shared sentience, then we are also the creators. Does that mean, in fact, we **are** creating our own reality? If so, then how we see each other is crucial. We must learn to see one another as Divine, rather than the infidel, the opponent, the victimizer. What would that mean? Could I see you are a Divine being if I see you with greed and wonton selfishness? I would have to be able to see past—or through—any negative attributes to a vision of your goodness, and you would have to see into mine. That would truly transform the world and all religious conflict.

It is not the power that makes one God—it is the presence. It is an energy that dissolves all separation, all loss, all questions. It does not overpower you, it envelops you and you return "home;" home to your very Source. Somewhere in your life you have enacted a godly deed of compassion, great love, mercy, healing, oneness. In that moment you activated your spiritual DNA. You not only "did" something through your earthly body, but you used your "essence" in pure energetic form. At that moment you were, in fact, God. Call it replication, imitation, second generation, or what you will, but you were irrevocably linked to the Divine Source, and you always will be. It is beyond anything you can devise to describe it or know it.

The lord of the Bible, the Torah, the Koran, was a lord of those times, but is it of our times? Are we ready for a new God whose covenants are different, a God who does not punish, a God who introduces us to the cosmos? I think we are. I am not saying we should say we don't believe in that god of old; I am saying we can discover the truth of a higher God who will teach us now.

That we are not alone in the universe will have a significant effect on our awareness, our perception of God in the near future. When we ask, "Who is God?" we answer that God is this one or that one, rather than God is all. Our relationship to the answer will be very, very different as we explore the cosmos and come to know that God is beyond personage, beyond form.

Jesus, Buddha and others each said in their own words, "I am the way, the truth and the light." All organized religion today would consider it absolute blasphemy if any of us were to say, "I am the way, the truth and the light"—yet we are. It isn't that we dare to think of ourselves as God, but we can allow our-selves—without the ego, without all of the conversation—to enact God, to live as God. I am not speaking of that lord of power and domination that we have had in the past, but of the Divine Christian love, the Buddhist compassion and any of the other attributes bestowed upon us through our spiritual DNA—through the kiss of life.

Who is God? You and you alone can answer this question. Let me whisper to you that your answer may change as you evolve into new truths. That is right and good! No one can take your god away from you; however, your perception and relationship to your god, like all your relationships, requires you to interact, to go beyond "automatic pilot" and participate—evolving that relationship in new ways.

Imagine if the cosmic energy of unconditional love, of healing, of manifestation, passed through **you**. You are Divine cosmic inheritance—not because you are a savior, not because you are powerful or someone special, but because you live. Your body is an instrument of that energy because it passes through you, whether you are aware of it or not. Don't think you have to be someone special to receive it or be worthy of it. It is your gift to extend into the world. It is the purpose, the destiny of your life. That is godly and that is who you are. All you have to do is choose it. Choose it, imagine it, practice it, and in so doing, it happens.

SIXTEEN

THE MESSAGE

THROUGH THIS BOOK, *THE EVOLUTION OF GOD*, I extend to you a message that is not born of intellect, or belief, but comes from an intrinsic spiritual source of my being—a place of the brilliant heart. The message is given through the filter of language, through the sieve of cosmic knowing, squeezed into the linear groove of writing from left to right. I know that some of my phrases might seem strange to you, but I hope you can let your mind capture or even create the images that I want to communicate. The words cannot bring forth the fullness of its meaning or breadth of the opening the message offers—yet I have extended it with the power of a true heart and I feel that such a heart can never be faulted.

I am saying that there is a Divine Source—not in the sense of a purely humanized consciousness, but rather an essential reference for life, evolution, for cosmic pulse, that allows all sentient beings to have a part in that universal energy. This universal consciousness, of which we are a part, sources our existence. The way we relate to it will inevitably evolve within the infinite play of cosmic potential. I call it "Divine" because it helps us to interpret its impersonal "goodness" as a sense of lovingness or relatedness that we can embrace and that embraces us—not exclusively, but through an essential relationship.

If we could perceive God as this infinite energy, we could heal our struggle about whether God is the only creator and the theory of evolution is wrong, or whether there is intelligent design orchestrating the universe. Each of these perspectives holds a part of cosmic truth and one day we will see that they actually intertwine.

The battles being fought over religious perspectives are exemplary of how we project our own emotional repertoire onto God. It is as if the adherents of different views are accusing the others of insulting God. God could not be insulted by the mind or emotions of men—they are too limited to ever enter a universal conversation.

We have always personified this Divine Source as a God of human dimension with emotions and demands clothed in our own expectations. It is time to let God evolve from the parental authority perpetually refereeing our squabbles, to the majesty of cosmic essence—untethered from our feeble sketch of the incomprehensible, infinite Divine Source that is beyond our comprehension.

If we washed away all the dogma and myths related to God, we could never lose the deepest essence of spiritual truth. Of course our forefathers personified God. Theirs was a world so small that every possible ripple seemed to be about them or came towards them. We still project out into the world our own presumptions and therefore create exactly what we expect, as did they. All our ancestors had was the power of the father, who commanded the family unit, and thus God fit exactly that role. The thought of separation from such a small reality was as frightening as death. Heaven provided an escape, a goal to leap across the finality of death.

The Divine Source offers the evolution of our Soul through multi-incarnational embodiment—a holographic array of life vignettes to bring enlightenment to our consciousness. As we become more enlightened, we will see them in simultaneous play so that we comprehend how our themes interface with each other across the web of lifetimes. The most important aspect of this is to see the thread from birth to death to birth so that we can overcome our primordial fear of extinction. The cosmos is not consecutive per se, not one reality of life and then another, but more like the big bang of holographic reality from which we can integrate energies that open up human experience to The Divine.

It is irrelevant whether we perceive our themes and experiences as composites of many lifetimes or the accumulation of psychogenetic inheritance down through generations. Our body holds them all in its cellular memory.

We have chosen to incarnate because of the profound opportunities it provides in both unmanifest and manifest worlds. Life is about growing our species into an enlightened group consciousness wherein we become aware of our human potential beyond what we have recognized to date.

Some of what was held true fifty years ago by "infallible" science has been proven untrue today. Why do we not see that some religious beliefs that were held true 2000 years ago are also not true today? There is no ultimate truth in the universe. In fact, truth can only be perceived through personal experience and that truth changes as we evolve. Instead of insisting upon some ultimate spiritual truth, we would gain more enlightenment by living the truths we recognize and seeing where they lead us. In terms of religion, we have blindfolded evident truths with the heavy fabric of faith.

We have put faith at the pinnacle of our religions and look where that blind faith has taken us? We are willing to continue the god wars that should have dissolved completely from our repertoire eons ago simply because we feel guilty about allowing our intelligence to help us discern what might or might not be true. The proselytizing that attempts to corral others into a certain religious point of view is not worthy of our consciousness or our humanity. It is smeared with the hidden agenda of the faithful thinking they are doing good for God. How many cultures have been despoiled by joining religions brought to them by the self-righteous supremacy of outside influences?

As our ability to think rationally and feel from more humane octaves advances, we could become aware of the cause and effect of our actions, and thus discern a higher truth. When we kill each other in the name of God, we turn against the essence of Divine Source. Blind faith without compassion and empathy has offered up fanaticism of the worst kind. It is time to temper faith with knowledge and spiritual oneness. Let us have faith in Divinity, rather than doctrine!

No one is innately less or more spiritual than any other because our spirituality is part of the human genome (which includes our spiritual DNA even if it has not been isolated), not a result of what we do. One person may consciously focus on spiritual realms and activities as their pursuit in life, while another may pursue "the good life." Each has a purpose that we cannot know without access to the holographic history of their Soul; therefore, judgment of others is contrary to spiritual law.

Even if one is an avowed atheist, it does not mean that he or she lacks spiritual essence. Such a person may be totally enraptured by a starry night that opens their consciousness to the cosmic flow. This is as profoundly a spiritual experience as is praying to a godhead.

The interminable debates about God verses science, creation verses intelligent design, are impotent distractions from what is important to our spiritual awakening. Perhaps this is why the voice of the feminine is so necessary now. It is essential that we focus on amplifying the "experience" of divinity in our lives without killing it with words or polluting it with hatred. If we could touch the sacredness of life the way every mother does, we would be willing to let others relate to the Divine Source in their own way, without belittling or trying to prove them wrong. Our oneness of spirit is the commonality of all great spiritual teachings.

We cannot know the limits of God. We cannot hold all its forms in our consciousness because our reference point is only here on earth. We have yet to transverse the heavens of the astral plane or the heavens of space itself. Our search will never end, just as will our Souls eternally renew themselves in the womb of The Divine. Let God grow! Let consciousness reach out beyond human loneliness and touch the **source** of the human being—the Divine Source.

What if we entered the conversation of participating as Source ourselves? Not only are we Divine because we are the miracle of life, but we are the Source of everything we attract to ourselves. When will we allow what comes to us to be positive, wonderful energies returning as the amplification of our mirroring divinity? We need the courage to imagine and practice Divine expression. We can argue about God forever, or we can activate the process of becoming godly, now.

Perhaps it is hard for you to imagine that you are a godly being. Would it be easier to imagine that you are a galactic and that your human self is a part of your repertoire as a living sentient being in a solar system, a galaxy, in a universe? Walk through this world as if you were one of the galactics of higher nature that has come to amplify beauty, to make things good, to help humanity evolve. You can do this. In fact, all people can do it because each person has within them the goodness and the power to participate in our evolution. Some Souls are here suffering from illness, hunger, poverty and other depravities so that others can awaken to higher spiritual truths—such as "what happens to you, happens to me." Which is the more Divine? They are not less spiritually advanced or even less powerful—perhaps to the contrary, their courage to be the object of the lesson is invaluable to the evolution of us all.

There is a difference between holding on to God and expressing God. We have been holding on so tightly to one facet of the Divine Source that we have all but strangled the voices that would bring enlightened awareness into our reality.

The God Source will eternally exist, but we desperately need to embrace its essence in new ways in order to avert our own demise through god wars that have so perverted our higher nature. As we have evolved into a more painful era of sense of self, we feel essentially alone, which causes us to cling to old ways that give us someplace to belong.

Our infinite Souls are present when we are squeezed from the "One Soul" into the individuated prick of spirit that initiates life. From the moment of conception, we often feel the sense of separation and limitation, rather than the ecstasy of creation. The human experience is overwhelming from the first jolt of human consciousness, lost in the minuscule reality of embodiment. This is only because we have not learned to hold the curtain of multidimensional reality open. We are beginning to do that now, but the cosmic view is petrifying to many.

Human consciousness has the innate capacity to touch The Divine through the facets of its multidimensional awareness. We must revisit the magic of such inexplicable experiences that carry us through the veil into other dimensions where we can feel its presence. All of us entered these places as children when we saw auras and spoke to wondrous beings, but which were later erased from our awareness. We can have a direct interface that infuses the communication with bliss and rapture. Historic tales of this phenomenon have been sung down through the ages. We have simply forgotten that it is our song.

No one wants to appear strange or feel the awkwardness of a spirituality that is not within the confines of approval of a collective understanding. Certainly we have also inherited the frightening psychogenetic imprints of being burned at the stake and other consequences of visible spiritual qualities. It has always been like that at a point of critical mass when we are on the verge of something entirely new. Almost all cultures fear the judgment of others. **Do not be afraid.**

In the same way that religions themselves evolve into new ones that break away from the old and rearrange and reconstruct what they think is true, we must be willing to do this en masse—and we are ready to do it now. It is time to say no to the concepts of infidels and sinners, heretics and dissidents, the excommunicated and the dammed. It is time to unshackle our minds and allow the visionaries and the pure of heart to speak of The Divine—not just the men or the learned, but the loving and the beloved.

Deeply seated loyalty issues come into play when we even imagine changing our religious practices or religious faith. A "God Almighty" would have no need for jealousy or loyalty expressed in religious practice above the universal laws of oneness. It could never be disloyal to the Divine Source to applaud all religions and support everyone who sees that life is an opportunity of Divine expression. It is our responsibility to insist that our religions uphold their sacred teachings—love, compassion, surrender, in every decree and action. If they do not, then it is evident that their deeper motives include greed and the quest for power.

The gods of our ancestors have come and gone. In what form and with what energy do we seek new ones today? None of the representations of the lord, of the god we have had in the past, truly serve the future of humanity, because the violence, the manipulation, and the punishments associated with them are too devastating for evolving consciousness. I sometimes wonder if those psychogenetic imprints are so deeply entrenched in us that we may actually be addicted to their reality.

We need to orchestrate a new sense of a Divine Source that is without these kinds of human interplays. In short, we need new gods, new templates that can take us to the next level of cosmic awareness. Christ and Buddha gave us a glimpse, but we did not practice their examples. Instead, we made up human interpretations of how to reach their exalted worlds of heaven and nirvana. To do that, Buddhists attempt detachment from the world, while Christians and Muslims instill the sense of imperfection and necessity of salvation from our "badness."

Until we have freed ourselves from the poisonous concept of salvation and its underlying illusion that we are the unworthy, sinful subjects of a vengeful god force, we will never ascend to the full power of our human potential.

Life needs no salvation, it needs only the currents of evolution. We do not need to be saved; we need to be taught, we need to be illuminated. God did not make humans in such poor form as to have to save them or destroy them. These are old concepts. We may discover that humans are not the creation of one god, but rather the result of some kind of higher consciousness. An important step in changing our relationship with the Divine Source is simply to remove the negative concept of salvation from the equation. It has poisoned our vision of what it is to be an embodied human Soul and cast us into an abyss of delusion for too long!

God does not need our fear, our submission, our loyalty or any of the other discourses we receive from our religions— under the pretext of transmitting God's commands. Perhaps the most tragic result of these negative imprints is that we have not allowed ourselves the freedom to search for new experiences, prophets, or visions of God. We can begin now!

It is not within cosmic law that the voice of The Divine be heard so sparingly in disconnected, historic time only. Are we caught like the great civilizations of old in the elusive, expectant void between godly appearances? Is this why we instigate God wars and bicker like unattended children—because no direct guidance has come to help us feel the Divine presence? We cannot leave our spiritual reference to the dubious interpretations of men and cultures that only exist through the skeletal shadows of the past. Imagine the infinite cosmos waiting for our awakening.

All the Divine beings who have come to show us a glimpse of spiritual realities have lifted human consciousness up only to hear the thud of our crash as we returned to the ground of our own existence. They showed us mysterious worlds and profound cosmic truths, and we reduced them to battles over who is the true God or true religion or who is a saint worthy of God's acceptance. All of the Divine beings who have mirrored or brought God consciousness to our planet are part of our spiritual evolution. What we have done with their teachings has been a travesty.

If we could release them from the religions that were created in their names, of the dogma, the belief systems that were formulated through human interpretation, we could experience them in their spiritual essence. In that way we would feel no separation or fear, or perhaps even no preference one over another, because each of them gave us a teaching that has opened the window of potential for all humanity. When I think of Buddha, Jesus, Muhammed, etc., I think of their essence, not their form. Learn to meditate on essence and you will become the energy of The Divine.

Can we practice the power of Buddha's compassion, Jesus' love, Muhammad's surrender and the wisdom of other great beings that has been offered to us without stifling them in religious dogma? What would become of the preachers and religious leaders who are still perpetrating such religious laws that swallow up the original energies? They might transform into the true teachers they were meant to be. Shouting about sin and judgment, pleasing or displeasing God, is neither enlightening nor true; it is the sound of threat, of sorrow and of fear. It is the death rattle of the past.

True teaching is an embracing, encouraging unveiling of consciousness that opens the way to the essence of our humanity, wherein truth can grow and evolve just like the universe itself. In the end, it matters not the choices made by religious leaders of the past; what matters is the way we carry our spiritual truth into the future through the choices we make at this moment for ourselves. It seems unlikely that representatives of churches can make a significant leap into enlightened spiritual expression because they are bound to perpetuate the past. The evolution of our Souls is inevitably in our own hands. My Higher Self says that we must become our own teachers, our own healers, our own priests.

Beyond the confusion, the imbalance and the poison of religious dogma, we can still love, embrace, and seek God. We can move through our religious rituals, sing our prayers, embrace the part that we have designed for godliness in our daily lives, and still allow the evolution of God. We are coming into a time when the invisible realities can enter into our awareness and set us free. The structures of religion, along with the ways they impinge upon our cultures and societies, must go through the shift from outer symbolism, to inner experiential truth.

Ultimately, it is not about what is wrong with religions, it is about what we are free to create. Even the Divine Source must breathe new possibility into the cosmos. Imagine human religious images blasted from form into cosmic images—from man to God. What would it be like?

Let us become the **essence** of our religions, not their crystallized, antiquated structure. There will come a time when the Divine Source will not be about how we should live, but that how we live will reflect all of Divinity. When human consciousness is more enlightened, rules will not be necessary, inner guidance will be inherent, and life will include a profound sense of Godliness within all sentient beings. We will have accessed our birthright and activated our true destiny.

We can become the religion and the culture of "humanity." Its spiritual attributes of love and compassion, heroism and will, provide the ultimate resolution of our conflicts. We have lost the sense of transcendence that is such a great teaching about lifting above the fray. If we held the vibration of transcendence in our consciousness, we would feel the inner peace that could carry us over any barrier and on to a place of holographic enlightenment.

"Peace is a choice" we say at the Nizhoni School of Divinity— and it is true that we must *choose* to be conscious of the Divine Source, or not. The grace of spiritual life is not about praying or meditating, studying or learning, it is truly about choosing. Once we do, the illumination begins to flow into our life unimpeded.

If we connected directly with our Divine Source, we would find that the effort in all levels of our lives would diminish. Instead of the struggle to drag our children to church, to entice our husbands and wives into weekly rituals, we would be free to feel the profound embrace of the cosmos in our hearts at every moment. Our minds would become illuminated with the wisdom we have sought for so long.

Time alters experiential truth—yet we have stubbornly refused to allow ourselves to see The Divine in new ways or even honor a higher octave of our humanity. World peace could be the most enlightened way to reflect the spiritual wisdom we have gained. Rather than the fear and struggle that swallows our small personal reality, we could embrace all humans as one Soul group and share peaceful existence as our birthright during this sojourn on earth. The gods of war who gained threshold into our evolution cannot continue because they divide humanity by domains and have not taught us peace— we must teach ourselves.

Whether it is one face of the Divine Source we recognize as God, or many personifications, really does not matter. They are only reflective of our own capacities and repertoire. How we transcend our lives now, how we bring the mysteries of the universe into our bodies and our world, is the next octave of all spiritual endeavors.

We are actually free to express and experience our relationship with the God Force in entirely new ways. There are aspects of ourselves that will emerge, which are unfathomable to us at this moment, but will soon become the core of our reality. We are Divine in essence and carry within our spiritual DNA the absolute potential to express that Divinity through our lives—on this plane. We do not yet know this potential in terms of its true meaning for our own evolution, but it can only be whole and embracing. If God is love, is love then not our own essence and our greatest truth? Our spiritual DNA will help us access skills such as healing, telepathy, bilocation, and awareness beyond our third dimensional reality.

Let us rid ourselves of the smallness of "it couldn't be me." The answer to this doubt is that it *has* to be us. It is the reason we are here. The fact is, we are related to God—whether we know it or not, whatever we do in life. All of our thoughts, feelings, choices, and expressions are the fodder for new possible Divine creations. "God grows through you," my Higher Self says.

A really thrilling possibility would be to see the Divine Source within its "own" context. How can we stretch our consciousness far enough to even imagine what that context might be? Possibly, the journey is an inward one into our purest core that we have not yet glimpsed.

Perhaps these thousands of years of Kali Uga (darkness) are but a flicker in the evolution of the Soul, and in fact, we are doing wonderfully well. We could be evolving into compassionate, merciful and loving, human beings. The evolution of God is actually the prerequisite of our own Soul evolution. We began with a word for Divine Source—we called it God. Then we claimed it and wielded it as a weapon. Now we are invited to extend our consciousness to discover new spiritual truths and this spiral will continue into infinity. As we go out into the universe, we will become enlightened as to cosmic laws, and through this knowing we will find new names and descriptions of what we have called—God. All things are transient, even beyond the universes. Our evolution does not have to be filled with turmoil and confusion; it could be filled with the power of transmutation, transfiguration, and transcendence.

We must let go of our past illusions so that we can be born into a world of comprehension of whom we are. What would it be like to look through the peephole into the cosmos and experience ourselves as energy, rather than as bodies?

Imagine yourself evolving into a truly godly being—filled with love and illumination. Imagine yourself transcending the limitations of your separate, lonely self—and the most breathtaking image of all—imagine that **you** are the key to "The Evolution of God!"

SEVENTEEN

QUOTES FROM
THE EVOLUTION OF GOD

To the Reader

"We dare dream of traveling beyond our planet, of miracles and magic—but we don't dare touch our god."

"Up until now on our planet we have experienced change as a threatening, dangerous and destabilizing energy that we resist within our families, our churches and our countries. However, change is what allows us to test the river of life, and find out what benefits the whole and what does not."

"We are in an eternal pulse of evolution—the evolution of our species, our consciousness and our Soul."

"It is time to sort through all of our belief systems and find the pearls of wisdom, the keys to joyous, ecstatic and free expression of our divinity."

"We cannot continue with our limited concepts of God. We cannot breed hatred and fear and war in the name of God. We must activate the intelligence of our hearts and—evolve God. This is not a sacrilege; it is our human right—and our responsibility."

Evolution: The Spiral of Perfection

"The motion of life penetrates a holographic field of energy, absorbing all its facets until it swings out to the periphery and spins itself up into a spiral—the spiral of evolution."

"If we hold the meaning of the word evolution to its developmental purpose of evolving into ever higher and more perfect states, then it becomes a tool of grace in our lives—a spiral of perfection."

"If the universe is ever changing, why do we think the Divine Source does not also evolve?"

"The truth of creation is that it continues onward; even words on a page will change their meaning as they are read and re-read."

"This is the mystery of consciousness wherein holographic experience synergistically designs truth."

"…we have left God back in a time capsule."

"…to persist in the illusion of an unchanging god is to place a wedge between the mind and the heart of modern believers."

"It seems unimaginable to contemplate the possibility that we could change God, even though that relationship has never, as yet, approached its full potential. It can not, until we free it from the constrictive prison of the human mind."

"Spiritual DNA is an illusive bundle of innuendos that hovers over the more palpable physical and emotional DNA. Together, they are interwoven into a cohesive whole that whispers back and forth across the veil of the unmanifest and completes the composition of who we are."

Chapter 1, Creating God: Fear to Sacrifice to Blame to Guilt

"Imagine the probability that the creator is itself touched by its creation as the energy streams out and returns through the fabric of interconnectedness, which then alters the potential of them both."

"Our perception is exploding into a horizon of brilliant palette and craves a new view of God—one without the smallness of human manipulation and projection—one which has integrated the magnificent teachings brought to humanity through all the prophets, seers and saints who have experienced or have been bestowed illumination through Divine focus."

"The church threatens with fear and then drives that sword so deeply into the human psyche that we are almost mortally wounded by the cut of God's anger and wrath."

"As our ancestors interacted with their world, they began to recognize a force of creation that seemed to hurl its power directly at them. When there was a storm or eruption, a trembling, or a great wind, they interpreted it as a personal act focused on them... Like their own explosions of fear and anger, they projected those energies of nature onto this colossal power that held their existence in its grip, and they gave it the name—GOD."

"Our relationship with God is not one directional, it is the dance of life."

"Now it is time to exponentially revise God into a consciousness that can help us to touch it even within the formless; to know that it is **we** who sculpt the form and voice of God in accordance with what we can perceive."

"Every new era must devise new forms of communion with the Divine Source so that the illumination furthers the advancement of our species."

"There are few enraptured audiences in church these days. Look around and you will detect the strain of patience during sermons, the flinch of guilt and head bowed in religious shame, but not the passion of joy to be focused on the Divine Source."

"The fear of God weighs so heavily upon us that we have not yet dared to truly explore the deepest truth—that we are each and all a part of the Divine Spark."

"Just as our children carry our attributes, so do we carry those of God."

"We have not fully understood the qualities of love and compassion that we can experience through the Divine template, and thus our world seems devoid of the goodness that was bestowed upon us through our spiritual DNA."

"What does it mean to be created by the Divine Spark? It means that we are here, in body, to be the vehicle of expression of a universal Soul."

"In our lifetime, we will witness that opening into a cosmic arena that will alter our concept of God and teach us new truths about life; we are not alone in the infinite sea of cosmic currents."

"It is our historical habit to wield God as a weapon in our battle with others as if our relationship to God would be threatened by the possibility that God would love them too."

"As the albatross is lifted, there will be a natural evolution of consciousness through which we can perceive the Divine Source in the light of expanded truth."

"Why would God ask for the destruction of its own creation? ...Only the machinations of primordial man could see this as true."

"In this instant of human history, the force of **blame** took hold as an attribute of responsibility and with it came the avoidance of being faulted."

"Whatever we are, is also our view of all else."

"God never gave a franchise to a selected few; you have the birthright of direct experience."

"It is as if all authenticity were frozen in a time capsule thousands of years old."

"It is not God who needs our compliance and obedience; it is the fabrication of our religions to bind us into a matrix of unified servitude."

Chapter 2, Evolving into Religions

"My Higher Self says that **the victim and the victimizer are one.** That means there is a spiritual connection between all beings and events."

"Justified violence in the name of God is an addiction that is deeply entrenched in the human psyche."

"Our genetic pool is so small that no one on the planet is further away from you than your forty-fourth cousin."

"There is a wealth of noble templates for martyrdom that lull us into the club of 'good guys.' …We need a new crop of human heroes who have not had to cast their lives into the dungeon of death to be remembered or honored."

"Lives lived under pretexts are unfulfilled lives of confusion, bound by the mind and entrapped by illusions of ancestry."

Chapter 3, The Crusades: Religion on the Move

"Politics and God have always been intertwined in the visions of the few and the submission of the many!"

"The Crusades, and all holy wars are a travesty against humanity and the sacredness of life!"

"The link between God and righteous struggle is so entrenched in our psyche that it is difficult to imagine that we can see past the superfluous banners of its pretense into the darkened spaces of its secret intent."

"Religious domination must become a thing of the past if we are to catch the next rung of the ladder and evolve as a species."

"In the encapsulated world of the fanatic, it is God that comforts and buries the hurt of being ostracized by assuring them that they are the righteous, the 'chosen' ones."

"Time, as we know it, *does* change truth! It is inextricably entwined with the wisdom of experience."

"Life—exposes and illuminates truth."

"Why do we linger with the God of the Crusaders, the God of the Israelites, Allah, or any of these violent ones who presumably demand war and death against the non-believers? No true God who has the power to create universes would ask these things."

"What lethal fog is this to think that God would be glorified by destroying Divine creation? We are only being exposed to a shadow form of The Divine—a filter clogged by the density of human thought and deed."

"We must dissolve our fear of dissention and the sanctimonies of the churches, so we can discard all remnants of our dishonest religious past."

Chapter 4, The Cross

"If we are an evolving species of Divine origin, then we need not carry with us into the future the limited concepts and conclusions of the constrictive past."

"Salvation is a concept bred of fear and intertwined with pain."

"Why would we be put into body just to be saved? No, we are here for a much more enlightened destiny."

"We have come to evolve and carry back to our Divine Source the fruit of our quest so that all manifest life could be enhanced by our infinite potential."

"Let us leap off this rung of the ladder wherein spiritual truth is eclipsed by the expediency of politics and power—as is still true today!"

"We have tethered ourselves to a negative version of aspiring to be godlike and placed the cloak of guilt around our burdened shoulders."

"Suffering is not Divine!"

"Peace and compassion between the Jewish and Christian faiths is paramount to a new world and the removal of the crucifixion theme will help us to refocus our attention onto the beautiful example he (Jesus) set for us all."

Chapter 5, Religious Concepts

"Free will is the gift of choice through which we sculpt experience into destiny."

"It is awareness of our evolutionary potential and its amplification that awaits our unedited creative flow."

"Let us be brave enough to accomplish the necessary changes within the adventure of new discoveries."

"The future generations of explorers will add new pieces to the God puzzle that may show us how to be a part of something much bigger than we have imagined!"

"We cannot be wrenched from God by any externalized judgment or wrongdoing because The Divine is the essence of beingness, not the doing."

"We continue with our religions not so much because we do not see the fallacies, incongruities and even deceptions, but because we need the sense of belonging, the comfort of habit, and the continuity of our cultures."

"We have yet to comprehend that The Divine is not a depository of the rational, but the energetic key to our essence."

"Our spiritual pain has been born squarely on the shoulders of our emotional and mind bodies."

"The swords of religion are the daggers of words and concepts that enforce emotional fear and intellectual righteousness, trouncing upon the trembling birth of our spiritual enlightenment."

"What would it be like to feel a beneficent, peaceful God within our bodies?"

"Independence is an unstable element in any institution and is carefully monitored by the 'powers that be.'"

"We do not have to find truth through suffering, nor do we need to be punished in order to learn how to be good."

"The laws of karma are always in play—the learning is the result of what occurs from the inside of our consciousness as we experience cause and effect—not from the outside."

"As we mature, inner knowing will release us from the grip of guesswork in terms of pleasing or obeying The Divine."

"Where salvation interfaces with forgiveness and freedom from guilt, it becomes a joyful sense of new beginnings."

"It is not such a terrible thing to free God from the role of father and instead take up the staff of authority ourselves."

"It is infinitely more magnificent to imagine a God that encompasses it all than a limited God whose sole domain is our present world."

"As we evolve, so will our relationship with the Divine source— all that is needed is our choice to expand our consciousness."

"God as a business is a lucrative endeavor; one that has been wielded with great success in virtually every society on the planet."

"There is a fine line between the investing and supporting of one's church and buying favors—to appease God, assuage guilt, annul marriages, receive indulgences, get into heaven and other negotiations through the mediation of church officials that are blatant manipulations of religious guidelines."

"The idea that God loves a poor person as a compensation for not having the basics of what one needs is a pretense for covering the inequalities that all institutionalized churches need to address."

"When we learn this lesson of sharing we will 'break bread' and humans will be ready to move to a new octave of manifesting abundance."

"The concept that money is not spiritual has become a point of great confusion in every culture."

"We need only to come to the realization that abundance is a form of grace to be shared and utilized for all, and that there is abounding joy connected to the giving."

"If we can move into a more experiential format and truly have the courage to look at those concepts that support us today, and those that do not, we will be able to bring religion with us into a new era of expanded reality."

Chapter 6, Molding the Masses

"The echoes of sin and judgment that have entrenched in our minds and hearts bind us to a false understanding of our creator."

"It is much easier to shout about the need to repent than it is to speak gently about our goodness."

"I have no doubt that our fearful, guilty minds have collectively created the eternal darkness of hell and the wrenching shadows of purgatory; but I have always known instinctively that it existed only by our own design—not God's."

"Yes, we are a young species, but we bring with us the wisdom of evolution, of Divine consciousness and the mandate to take responsibility for our realities and our world."

"Once we have been molded, we can see its effects in the subtle choices we make and the conclusions that follow. Consciousness of this molding process can untangle us from negative imprints and help us to free ourselves from the clutch of control."

"If religious doctrine has forged an indelible imprint of human frailty or evil, then we must find a way to break out of its mold or we will never discover the magnificent goodness we hold inside us."

Chapter 7, Churches Today

"A diet of unconditional love and consciousness is what we need now; it is the feast set before us by the great templates of Divine truth."

"It is time for us to stop atoning for the deeds of our ancestors. The only thing to lament here is that we may have inherited such negative imprints of humans."

"Despite the inhuman things we are still perpetrating against each other, we are goodness in our core and we are learning."

"The threats of old do not have as much power over us as they once did—perhaps we are so busy in the outer world that even hell will have to wait!"

"The Soul holds a blueprint of evolutionary growth for its incarnation, but the choice of how its lessons are learned is a part of free will."

"For some, death is the greatest healing—to return to the womb of the universe, having completed one round of the evolution of the Soul and come again into the embrace of the infinite."

"The balancing of karmic acts from this lifetime, and any other, need not be put into perspective through pain and punishment."

"If God neither punishes us nor saves us we might wonder: 'What is God's purpose in our lives?'"

"We are here on a mission: to transform humanity into an ever more magnificent expression of Divine potential."

"One day we will free ourselves from fear and separation, banish illness and perhaps even death through our own consciousness, and our prayers will become glorious exaltations to the Divine Source of which we are a part."

"Of course, it is comprehensible to pray for help when we feel helpless, but its motive is centered on the survival of the self, which is ultimately an impoverished view of universal truth."

"That which we can conceive, we know within our Soul."

"The purpose of our presence in body is to bring new possibility and creativity to the One Soul through the experience of embodiment."

"Our religions are just the pretexts we use to justify our destructive urges and our churches are all too often the breeding grounds for schooling hatred."

"Churches today must not be bound to the stakes of past human servitude and suffering, but must break free in order to shine light on all Divine possibility that could illuminate evolutionary leaps of perception into the great mystery of humans and their gods."

"… it is never God's will to hand us misfortune…"

"As we evolve, we will let go of our need for personalizing God and grow into the consciousness of cosmic love, which is not about our everyday lives but about the wholeness of our being."

"How fantastic it would be to pray for illumination, for the strength to solve our problems, for the sense of oneness. Like preventative medicine, we could use prayer to focus our consciousness on the possible solutions that could come to us."

"What would it be like to pray—**for** God?"

"Spiritual law holds that all endings are the source material of new beginnings—ad infinitum. If we understood this in our essence, we could truly 'surrender' to the flow. The Soul is eternal. We will never be lost."

"It is not the belief in God that needs to be undone, it is the antiquated interpretation of God that must now be left behind."

Chapter 8, God and the Book

"Our infinite possibility of knowing the God Source through our senses and consciousness has been eclipsed by the constrictive format of words that attempt to describe, but do not truly access, the Divine vibration."

"Spiritual experiences have been covered in the sands of words that not only reconfigured them, but changed the landscape of universality as well, by rooting **individuals** as the trees of truth."

"This idea that truth is cloistered in the form of words is with us today and will be, perhaps, tomorrow as well; we still believe the written word almost unequivocally."

"Ultimately, only we can assess for ourselves whether we find holy books of Divine origin or not."

"What we can do with the written texts is honor the wisdom our ancient religious books offer us, and at the same time, allow ourselves to pass through those parts that are so obviously inappropriate to our reality."

"Spiritual teachers who insist that every word of their books is that of God, deny the birthright of personal spiritual experience and intuitive knowing; they are frozen in the blinding dogma of religious storm."

"Perhaps there are layers of Divine consciousness, which will come into view as we expand. This need not neutralize our belief in one God, but rather allow our awareness to engage the many facets of such luminescence that are beyond our present intelligence."

"Imagine yourself as an enlightened being who could direct the actions of humans. What kind of commandment would you give?"

"Embrace your divinity always, and in all ways, live divinely. Speak and act as if you were the Divine Source. You are your Higher Self, the all-knowing, intuitive essence of your Soul."

"Witness the sacredness of life. See it in all beings. Know there is Divine purpose in each experience and in each life."

"Bring Divine consciousness into every aspect of your life. Wield your business, your body, and creative endeavors all from the spin point of your Soul."

"For all things, be grateful. True gratitude for all experience and all people, ultimately brings enlightened evolution."

"Use your body as a Divine vehicle. Learn to commune with it and it will bring you health, ecstasy and illumination."

"Entrain your mind to find possibility and potential in every dilemma. Your own Divine Source gives you access to all solutions."

"Always speak your truth from clarity and compassion, and give yourself permission to change that truth as you grow."

"Whatever you want, give that. If you want love, give love. If you want money, give money. If you want acknowledgement, give acknowledgement. It is the giver who creates."

"Balance the male and female energies within you so that each has powerful, yet gentle expression."

"Teach your consciousness to hold goodness and inspiration."

"… we must find the courage to move forward into a more enlightened awareness of The Divine, and for the sake of the future, change what needs to be changed."

"In today's world, we do not need teachings of war; we need examples of peace to lead us through a questionable future teetering on the precipice because of the human habit of fighting."

"I believe in the goodness of humans!"

"Religions cannot be based on writings alone. They must carry with them a sense of awe and essence that goes far beyond words. If we hold on to the words, we will ultimately find ourselves empty and without the Divine connection that is essential to life."

"We must learn how to become enlightened beings who can manifest and wield energy without suffering."

"In the end, our spiritual evolution is not what is written in a book, and it is not even what is said, nor who said it. Rather, it is how we take a message or teaching that inspires us, that allows us to feel our connection to The Divine, and how we bring that into our lives, becoming what we truly are—beings of Divine Source."

"…Come beyond your books—come into the heart of humanity where God truly dwells. If you touch that place, you will become the truest essence of all you have ever read."

Chapter 9, Women and The Divine

"It is a gift of feminine consciousness to allow growth, rather than choose its particulars and force them upon another."

"There is no question in my mind that men in antiquity created God in **their** image so they could relate to such an incomprehensible energy through the blinders of their conceptual faculties."

"The energy of mothering is sacred because it nurtures the Divine ovum and brings it into the world, growing it into the future generation."

"Virtually all monotheistic religions have cast sexuality into the abyss of sin against God, or at least spun a thick web of taboos around it, subtly entrapping women in its midst."

"Each and every one of us has the right to embrace our religion in all aspects of our life."

"It is time that women and men alike, who hold the psychogentic inheritance of intuitive and loving spiritual essence, step forward and awaken to the reality that we must learn to honor each other. Our cultural realities have eclipsed our essential humanity—one Soul family that has come to earth to transcend and evolve."

"We need to bring all of the magic into our common domain within the routine of our everyday realities."

"All of us, males and females, have psychogenetically inherited from the Goddess the undeniable power of feminine knowing, intuition, and clairvoyance. We need to live the wisdom we have inherited within our spiritual DNA so we can open onto a cosmic universe beyond such minuscule details as we perceive in this moment."

"Let the women come forward and open the threshold to the center of the Soul!"

Chapter 10, God and Sexuality

"Nothing separates us faster from the sense of sacredness than the conversation of sexuality!"

"It is time we changed our obsolete views of sexuality so that our religious awareness can truly enter into the world in which we live."

"It seems necessary to understand sexuality from a more holographic perspective than just its enactment."

"Let us begin a new era of sexual expression in which we are truly ourselves—without the play of guilt or fear or shame."

"Let us be conscious that our sexual energy is mysterious and Divine, and that these qualities can be mixed into the experience of it in the physical, so that through sexual expression, we are transformed."

"Let us make love with delicious joy, with all our hearts, and for the purpose of oneness."

"Let us once again use our sexual energies as an avenue to the Divine Source!"

Chapter 11, Tracking Your Own Spiritual Repertoire

"Tracking your own spiritual repertoire will be a fascinating exploration of your spiritual roots and help you to see many aspects of your familial and cultural self that you may not have been aware of. In doing this, you will open new avenues of spiritual conversation within yourself and also with your relatives. You will be helping everyone around you through this process."

Chapter 12, The Technology of Consciousness: Exercises

"We may blanket ourselves in the comfort of our faith or beliefs, but all the while we sense an immovable block that separates us from a powerful energy we know is there somewhere. We want to reach it and at the same time we are terrified to even question whether it exists."

"We all want to live in a more enlightened spiritual world, but we do not know how to make the changes necessary to do it. We have never found a way through our minds, emotions (or our religions) into a place of clarity and connection to our own spiritual truths, most of which reside just on the other side of our conscious awareness."

"I created this 'technology of consciousness' to help us truly release the blockages that keep us from being free of restrictive belief systems and the fears they engender in us."

"There are infinite points within the matrix of our multidimensional bodies that are triggered through association and encoded reference, which engineer not only our genes, but also the structure of our reality. We can access them consciously and energetically to free ourselves from those that hold us in repetitive karmic patterns."

"The physical body is made of light, and therefore light is the best language of communication between our consciousness and the mind of the cell."

Chapter 13, God and Reincarnation

"We can actually alter the future by changing the remnants of the past that are crystallized in our phychogenetic patterns."

"One of the obstacles to our enlightenment of the cosmos is our confusion of linearity and the constriction of time on a continuum. It is almost impossible for us to comprehend that 'past lives' are going on now—that time pulses and is spatial, but is not simply a linear thread."

"In the same way that our childhood set the perimeters of who we think we are in the present, the imprints of the 'past' relive themselves through repetition until we have mastered or become illuminated through those experiences—irrespective of the number of embodiments."

"We think of reincarnation through the view of the body, rather than that of the Soul. If we could see its value in terms of Soul evolution, we could advance our consciousness in catapultic leaps."

"The cosmos will always depend on matter to frame the unmanifest. We will always exist."

"Through awakened consciousness we will be able to use the power of transfiguration from one level of cosmic existence to another with the grace of mastery. It is our true potential and we can begin now!"

"If heaven and hell are places we go after our lives, from what place do we come?"

"I would offer that heaven is a state of consciousness; one that can be entered at any moment—not simply after death or before life."

"Those you have hurt by your thoughts or actions need to be rebalanced through your conscious awareness so that you can expand your own hologram of positive potential— and above all, free yourself, and them, from the vicious cycle of repetition."

"There is a recognizable power in perceiving the hologram of action and reaction."

"As we experience life from all points of the hologram, we evolve because we have the gamut of reference from the victim to the victimizer and all the players in-between."

"No, we do not 'burn in hell' forever. The dastardly deeds of one lifetime cannot stop the pulse of infinity and are eventually rebalanced by their opposites of compassion and goodness in other incarnations."

"What would happen if you saw through the veil into the astral sleeve of lifetimes and focused your themes on God and spirituality? I am sure that you would begin to see beyond the content of those incarnations into levels of profound essence in which you could find new meaning for life."

"Each illumination that comes to our consciousness gives us access to even greater possibilities, not only in terms of knowing God, but also who we are and what we can become."

"It seems logical that any 'second coming' of a god figure would never be a repetition of the old. We have been waiting for something that is already transcended."

"It is not the power shown over matter or life that makes one God—it is the presence of Divine Source, the ultimate genesis of the self and the cosmos."

"We will forever come forth from the unmanifest into the manifest worlds so that what we gather through physical focus can be offered back to further the evolution of the Divine Source."

"When we truly know that consciousness is not entrapped in body, that we will always survive, then we will reach out with the curiosity and sense of exploration necessary to open new worlds."

Chapter 14, Gods and Galactics II

"Gods and Galactics is a discussion we can only have if you are willing to explore the possibility that we are not alone in the great cosmos of universes."

"If we realize that we are truly part of the vast cosmos, we might begin to experience a sense of spiritual oneness that will take us beyond the constrictions of form."

"Our concept of God must evolve to embrace the knowledge of the infinite Divine Source beyond human form and reference."

"Consciousness is not entrapped in our human DNA. It needs not breath, no arms, legs or ears. It can move between old and new bodies, be shared or superimposed onto something else, instilled into any kind of matter while it permeates the entire cosmos."

"If we can begin to think of 'God' in terms of pure consciousness instead of as the template of our own form, we will be

ready to discover possibilities that have not come to our awareness in the past."

"Our children's children will travel out beyond our solar system and will not only marvel at the infinity of the Divine
Source, but also about how we could not see what for them
will be so obvious—our perception of God was too small!"

"How convenient to wield the title of God over those who
have no comprehension of what is really happening."

"Earth is a body in a solar system, within a galaxy, within a
universe—therefore, we are all galactic beings, by definition."

"It is time for us to remove the stigma of sci-fi from the galactic conversation, because our future includes galactic connections—without a doubt."

"The question is not if we are of galactic origin, but how can
we harvest the potential it offers us if we become aware of it?"

"Who were those gods who demanded the hearts of the pure
and the brave? —Not the kind we want!"

"Psychogenetic imprints have been laid down within us all as
to how we imagine God."

"It must always be our intuitive knowing that allows us to feel
truth within the energetic qualities of higher beings that we
can trust."

"What we can trust is that we are on the brink of discoveries
that will sever forever the concepts we have had about the

God Force, and that we will have the most profound opportunity to free ourselves from the constrictions that held us back from experiencing divinity as an essence we share with all life, whatever its form or origin."

Chapter 15, Who is God? A New Sense of the Divine Source

"The Divine Source is pure light, infinite consciousness and the ever evolving, yet constant of all manifest and unmanifest dimensions."

"The future holds incomprehensible realities for us and it behooves us to stretch out to meet it, rather than refuse to imagine 'The Evolution of God.'"

"Beyond time and the laws of life we comprehend, there exists a creative flow that is expressed in incalculable forms, sculpted by a multi-faceted, conscious energy."

"What if it were that when we prayed, we were indeed praying to the God within us, to the godly essence of which we are a part, so that we magnified and caused that for which we prayed—rather than an outside, unconnected power answering our prayers."

"...the Divine essence holds its power and its truth from within us."

"Use the name you wish and clothe The Divine in any form, but it will always remain above confines of description."

"The ancient texts are addressed to those within the eras of their delivery and much of their context is detrimental to the awakening of our consciousness now."

"Everywhere in our lives exists the spiritual initiations that offer us illumination and greatness. They are often concealed in everyday experiences and we do not recognize them as such, so they slip by like the proverbial turning of the wheel of karma, and we miss our evolutionary opportunity because we do not see the connection."

"The Divine Source lives within each and all humans, and every one of us has the choice to use that Source to evolve our lives and our world."

"Our universal spiritual connection is what should bring us together, not the form or belief systems in which we dress it."

"It is not plausible or even possible to imprison the future of God only because we wish, or have been told, that there will be no change or evolution."

"It is not the power that makes one God—it is the presence. It is an energy that dissolves all separation, all loss, all questions. It does not overpower you, it envelops you and you return 'home;' home to your very Source."

"Somewhere in your life you have enacted a godly deed of compassion, great love, mercy, healing, oneness. In that moment you activated your spiritual DNA. You not only 'did' something through your earthly body, but you used your 'essence' in pure energetic form. At that moment you were, in fact, God."

"Are we ready for a new God who introduces us to the cosmos? I think we are."

"Who is God? You and you alone can answer this question."

"Imagine if the cosmic energy of unconditional love, of healing, of manifestation, passed through you."

"You are a Divine cosmic inheritance—not because you are a savior, not because you are powerful or someone special, but because you live."

Chapter 16, The Message

"I am saying that there is a Divine Source—not in the sense of a purely humanized consciousness, but rather an essential reference for life, evolution, for cosmic pulse, that allows all sentient beings to have a part in that universal energy."

"It is time to let God evolve from the parental authority, perpetually refereeing our squabbles, to the majesty of cosmic essence—untethered from our feeble sketch of the incomprehensible, infinite Divine Source that is beyond our comprehension."

"Let us have faith in divinity, rather than doctrine!"

"Life is about growing our species into an enlightened group consciousness wherein we become aware of our human potential beyond what we have recognized to date."

"There is no ultimate truth in the universe. In fact, truth can only be perceived through personal experience and that truth changes as we evolve."

"Instead of insisting upon some ultimate spiritual truth, we would gain more enlightenment by living the truths we recognize and seeing where they lead us."

"In terms of religion, we have blindfolded evident truths with the heavy fabric of faith."

"We have yet to transverse the heavens of the astral plane or the heavens of space itself. Our search will never end, just as will our Souls eternally renew themselves in the womb of The Divine."

"Let God grow!"

"What if we entered the conversation of participating as Source ourselves?"

"We need the courage to imagine and practice Divine expression."

"We can have a direct interface that infuses the communication with bliss and rapture. Historic tales of this phenomenon have been sung down through the ages. We have simply forgotten that it is our song."

"It could never be disloyal to the Divine Source to applaud all religions and support everyone who sees that life is an opportunity of Divine expression."

"It is our responsibility to insist that our religions uphold their sacred teachings—love, compassion, surrender, in every decree and action."

"Life needs no salvation, it needs only the currents of evolution."

"We do not need to be saved, we need to be taught, we need to be illuminated."

"God did not make humans in such poor form as to have to save them or destroy them."

"God does not need our fear, our submission, our loyalty, or any of the other discourses we receive from our religions—under the pretext of transmitting God's commands. Perhaps the most tragic result of these negative imprints is that we have not allowed ourselves the freedom to search for new experiences, prophets, or visions of God. We can begin now!"

"Imagine the infinite cosmos waiting for our awakening."

"Learn to meditate on essence and you will become the energy of The Divine."

"In the end, it matters not the choices made by religious leaders of the past; what matters is the way we carry our spiritual truth into the future through the choices we make at this moment for ourselves."

"Even the Divine Source must breathe new possibility into the cosmos. Imagine human religious images blasted from form into cosmic images—from man to God. What would it be like?"

"We can become the religion and the culture of 'humanity.'"

"If we connected directly with our Divine Source, we would find that the effort in all levels of our lives would diminish. Instead of the struggle to drag our children to church, to entice our husbands and wives into weekly rituals, we would be free to feel the profound embrace of the cosmos in our hearts at every moment. Our minds would become illuminated with the wisdom we have sought for so long."

"World peace could be the most enlightened way to reflect and touch God."

"Rather than the fear and struggle that swallows our small personal reality, we could embrace all humans as one Soul group and share peaceful existence as our birthright during this sojourn on earth."

"How we transcend our lives now, how we bring the mysteries of the universe into our bodies and our world, is the next octave of all spiritual endeavors."

"Our evolution does not have to be filled with turmoil and confusion, it could be filled with the power of transmutation, transfiguration, and transcendence."

World peace could be the most enlightened way
to reflect and touch God.

ABOUT THE AUTHOR

Spiritual Teacher, Healer, and Visionary, Chris Griscom, has authored fourteen books that have been translated into thirteen languages on subjects of spirituality, health, and human potential. She was opened to the awareness of our *eternal* Soul through her profound experiences of life and death during nine years in the Peace Corps. As a result of a life changing spiritual experience, she founded the church of The Sanctuary of Light and The Nizhoni College of Divinity. She also founded The Light Institute of Galisteo, an internationally prestigious spiritual healing center in Galisteo, New Mexico. Chris is a world renowned authority on reincarnation and teaches about the Soul's evolution through embodiment.

Chris Griscom has devoted her life to the development of spiritual technology, the expansion of consciousness and the evolution of the Soul. She travels the world giving talks and seminars, while continuing her work at The Light Institute.

OTHER WORKS BY CHRIS GRISCOM

BOOKS

Time is an Illusion

Ecstasy is a New Frequency:
Teachings of The Light Institute

The Healing of Emotion

The Ageless Body

Feminine Fusion

Nizhoni: The Higher Self in Education

Quickenings: Meditations
for the Millennium

Soul Bodies

Psychogenetics: The Force of Heredity

Words of Light

BOOKS ON CD

Soul Bodies

The Healing of Emotion

The Ageless Body

Feminine Fusion

Time is an Illusion

BOOKS ON TAPE

Psychogenetics: The Force of Heredity

Ecstasy is a New Frequency:
Teachings of The Light Institute

DVDs

Knowings with Chris Griscom

Yoga in the Garden

Chris Griscom: Live and Unedited

The Ageless Body

VIDEO TAPES

Window to the Sky I:
Light Institute Exercises

Windows to the Sky II:
Connecting with Invisible Worlds

The Ageless Body

Death & Samadhi

AUDIO TAPES

Transcending Adversity

Death & Samadhi

Sense of Abundance

The Gift of Peace

The Dance of Relationships/
La Danza de las Relaciones

The Creative Self

Knowings

Desert Trilogy

The Light Institute
40 Calle Nizhoni
Galisteo, NM 87540 USA
Telephone: 505-466-1975
Fax: 505-466-7217

thelight@lightinstitute.com
www.lightinstitute.com
www.chrisgriscom.com